# RAISED BY WOLVES

*Trapped by Demons*

Mimi Tallo

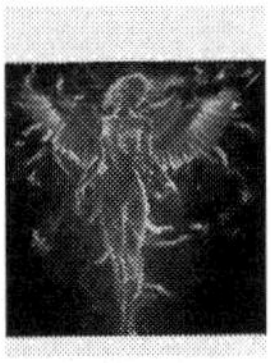

To Marilee
A light in the darkness, always. A rock who is there for everyone. Love, Love, love.

Mimi

*This book could not be written without the emotional support from my psychologist Katie Skopp, the spiritual support from Rev. Taylor Stevens, or the loving support from my husband, Jerry Brier.*

*"Whenever something negative happens to you, there is a deep lesson concealed within it. "*

ECKHART TOLLE

# CONTENTS

# FOREWORD

This is my story about coming into the world feeling unloved and unwanted. Raised by an alcoholic father and a cold detached mother, I had to make my way in the world based solely on my instincts.

My childhood would not include piano lessons, tap dancing and Girl Scouts. I would start working at nine years old. A good student and lover of literature, I aspired to be a teacher. That path was not made available to me. Instead, my parents expected me to remain at home and provide them with additional income. I felt trapped. My escape routes through the years included men, alcohol and drugs.

A victim of childhood abuse, sexual and physical assault, I learned to accept the unacceptable in order to survive.

A major pattern of self-destructive choices began to emerge. A significant portion of my life was spent uncovering, forgiving, and trying to resolve that pattern. I had decades to live before I would comprehend the predestination of my journey.

Set against the background of Scranton Pennsylvania and West Palm Beach Florida, included are numerous historical facts about both areas. There are stories of the gangsters in our town, specifically soldiers connected to the Buffalino family. There are details about highly publicized murders, famous politicians and business kingpins. My story is told against the backdrop of the chauvinistic culture of that time. Revealing what it was like mistakenly thinking women might get ahead because of the Women's Liberation Movement. The reality of my world was sexual objectification and condescension.

After four decades of self-detrimental behavior, three divorces, psychoanalytic treatment, stopovers at inpatient facilities, counseling and 12 Step programs, I finally found a little happiness. What I didn't find was joy. Sobriety had revealed that I was still emotionally numb. The trauma of my life still lurked in the shadows of my psyche.

Polish psychologist Dr. Kazimierz Dabrowski realized that the common nature / nurture debate was missing something. It had overlooked the role that we play in our own development. He called this 'The Third Factor.' The will to keep living life no matter what it might generate.

The intention of writing the bare unadorned truth of my life is to be an example to women that are being abused in any way. I want to reveal to other marginalized women to never give up. My goal is to ignite the desire to live and grow in others. You can weather post-traumatic stress and psychological issues if you have the Third Factor.

***"Life is inherently risky. There is only one big risk you should avoid at all costs, and that is the risk of doing nothing." Denis Waitley***

# INTRODUCTION

Human beings are meant to feel emotion. When that mechanism is short-circuited, first by emotionally neglectful parents and later continued by bad choices as an adult, it throws off the whole organism. Depression and anxiety are two of the most common causes of emotional numbness. Trauma and addiction were also on my personal hit parade.

Many years of counseling, soul searching and gut-wrenching honesty have started to dissipate that numbness. I was able to break free from most of my demons. I no longer feel trapped. I now have many moments of happiness and a few glimpsess of joy. Progress not perfection is my maxim.

# PREFACE

A major portion of my life has been spent uncovering, forgiving, and resolving my self destructive patterns. I wrote this book for the still marginalized women in this world. I have been a victim, a survivor and today an imperfect but integrated spiritual being. Putting on paper the bare unadorned truth of my life is both frightening and freeing.

# PROLOGUE

I guess you repeat some version of what you grew up with. My mother was cold, introverted and detached. I have no memories of her ever hugging or kissing any of us. My brother Joe said she would tie him up in the basement and hit him with a hose. She told him her life would be much better if he had not been born.

She would work all day in a factory and come home after my father had left for the night shift. It is a mystery to me how they found time to conceive four children. I neither have good or bad memories of my mother from when I was a child. I have read that a mother's role is that of a mirror, reflecting who the daughter is. A reflection of her strengths, talents, fears, and her hopes for the future. As a result of not looking into a maternal mirror, I grew up feeling unseen and misunderstood. I suffered from low self-esteem and a high degree of self-doubt.

Plato uses the allegory of the cave as a way to discuss the deceptive appearances of things we see in the real world. He encourages people to instead focus on the abstract realm of ideas and dreams and not on the darkness. No matter how dark my life became, I just keptgoing toward the light.

Some people never come out of the cave.

# CHAPTER 1

# POWERLESS

This wasn't my first time in a therapist office.  I had been in therapy for marriage counseling and had dabbled with suicidal ideation. This was different. I had just been released from Marworth Treatment Center for addiction. The psychiatrist at the Rehab told me that I was dual diagnosed and cross-addicted.  I guess that meant I can be addicted to anything, which is probably true.

The official diagnosis was cross-addiction, chronic depression and anxiety disorder. It was revealed to me that the 20 years I spent in addiction , was a form of self-medication. Until the cure became worse than the illness, and I hit an emotional and spiritual bottom.

I was apprehensively waiting to see the psychologist. I was hoping he was not as gruff as the psychiatrist I had to see before I could start therapy.

Dr. Boriosi was a well-respected psychiatrist in our

area. His bedside manner, however, left something to be desired. I needed to see him for the meds I would need.

Dr. Lemon entered the room and shut the door gently. We first made some small talk and summarized my recent stay in Rehab. The doctor seemed like a very loving, caring soul.

His office was very inviting with a big overstuffed chair and a couch with lots of pillows. A painting by Degas hung on one wall. His various degrees in Psychology hung on another.

He asked me to start with my earliest memory. I said I have many black holes in my memory. Dr. Lemon told me remembering is a spiritual experience. We are here on earth to remember our identity. Memories may come back later or not at all. He said that is okay, just tell me what you can remember. What's your earliest memory?

My earliest memory was when I was 5 years old and looking forward to kindergarten. Instead, I, with my brother, was dropped off at an orphanage. Dad took us to this big building with women that were dressed all in black with white around their faces. I later found out it was St. Joseph's Orphanage.

Mother Crescentia, Sister of the Immaculate Heart of

Mary had founded it in 1890. There was a growing problem of deserted children in the city of Scranton. Many fathers died in mine accidents and the widows could not take care of the children. There are not many details about the abandonment of these children. This IHM order immediately organized a home for abandoned children and adopted the name, St. Joseph's Society for Orphans.

My mother was in the hospital giving birth to my brother Matt, the third sibling. I guess family relationships between us and our maternal grandmother were strained at the time. They felt they had no one to take care of us two, while she was in the hospital. My mother had four sisters who she could have called on to help.

Now I know it sounds strange. It's always seemed strange to me. Can you imagine at 5 years old, being left at an orphanage? My father left us with the nuns and said he'd be back in a little bit. Ironically, this was the same orphanage that my father lived in for the first four years of his life.

It was really disconcerting when the nuns told us our clothes were too nice compared to the other children. They took our clothes and gave us old tattered clothing. I remember well, because they were scratchy, probably wool. They told us the boys and girls must be separate.

They took my brother away. I remember that night sleeping in a bunk bed with another little girl.

In the morning we lined up to use the bathroom. Breakfast was thin, watery oatmeal and lunch was a soft-boiled egg and toast. Then we were herded out to the playground. I saw my brother Joe. He ran to me and hugged me so hard, I almost fell to the ground.

The next day my father came to visit us. He brought us each a Hershey bar. The Sister took them and said we could have them after dinner. We never saw a piece of those candy bars. Although it felt like an eternity, my parents allege it was only 5 days.

For some unknown reason they also decided that I should not go to kindergarten. Whenever I see the poster " All you need to know you learned in kindergarten", I get pissed. I don't remember much of my childhood years after that.

I do remember walking home from school with my brother Joe. There was a crossing guard we called Joe the cop, even though he wasn't a cop. He seemed to like us more than the other kids. Anyway, I vaguely remember him inviting us to stop by his house one day after school. We did and he gave us candy. That's all I remember, it seems inconsequential.

A few days later he came to our house. He was drunk. He knocked on the door. Told my father that he had a beautiful daughter and that he better take care of her. I remember my father getting very angry and that was it. That's all I remember.

At that point in my story, I shrugged my shoulders and let out a sigh. Dr. Lemon took that moment to tell me there was such a thing as disassociated amnesia. Sometimes you have things in your life that you don't want to remember. The brain can just put them in cold storage. "That's makes sense" I remarked. Dr. Lemon told me to please continue.

Joe and I used to walk home every day from school on Pittston Ave, the main thoroughfare through Southside.

We walked the last two blocks to our house alongside Pittston Avenue Cemetery. It was the German Presbyterian Church Cemetery. It had a wall that we would climb up and then walk on top of the wall. At the end of that corner was Brook Street and it was very steep. At the bottom was a creek.

Brooks are typically smaller and shallower than creeks. This was a wide and deep body of water, definitely not a brook. I don't know why they didn't call it Creek Street. I guess Brook just sounded nicer.

Behind that creek was a wooded area that we called Cow Hill. Joe and I used to love playing on Cow Hill. We built forts and hideaways. We also would like to play in the alleys behind our homes with other neighborhood kids. You mostly stuck to your own block.

My house was on Pittston Ave and it was bordered by Brook and Cherry Street and then the bottom street was Cedar Avenue. My brother and I could do anything if we stayed on the block.

The weekends in my house were especially nightmarish. On Fridays when we reached home after school, we held our breath and opened the front door. If my father had a glass of beer in front of him, we knew it was going to be hell for the weekend. If there wasn't a glass of beer, we sighed a sigh of relief.

My father was a binge drinker. Monday through Friday he would work the night shift at the Capitol Records Factory. Some weekends he would cut grass for people to make extra money. If there was a weekend when there was no grass to cut, then he would prefer to drink. He was jovial for the first couple of hours, but then came the witching hour we all dreaded.

We would lay in our beds and wait to see whose name would be called. Usually, he would start with my mother. We would hear them at the kitchen table, mostly hearing my father shouting and pounding the table.

Then he would call one of two names. He would either call Marie or Joe. If he called Joe, it was a shorter ordeal, but a horrible hell. At some point I would hear him take off his belt. He would beat my brother and then send him back to bed.

If he called Marie, it was a seemingly never-ending hell. He would talk endlessly about his childhood, how he had been wronged and humiliated by his family. After an hour or so, he would look at me and say "If looks could kill I would be dead. There is such hate coming from your eyes". He eventually would fall asleep and I would scurry off to bed.

Dr. Lemon asked, "How did all this make you feel when you were a child. Did you think it was normal behavior?" I told him what my parents told me "What happens in your house stays in your house". I never even thought about telling a teacher or a priest. He asked me again, how did that make you feel?

I answered in Italian: "Lui ha il potere e io non ne ho"

I felt powerless.

# CHAPTER 2

# CHINESE FIRE DRILLS

Driving home from Doctor Lemon's office, I started to think about my father's childhood. His father had immigrated from Ribera Sicily. Ribera is a small community near Palermo. It was founded in 1630 by Prince Luigi Mogdano and named Ribera, his wife's surname. My Grandfather Giuseppe Tallo was born in Ribera in 1888.

I was told that side of my family has been around since the time of Julius Caesar. The family historian and scholar, also named Matteo, traced us back to a Tallo that was one of Julius Caesar's secretaries.

No one before my grandfather or since has immigrated to the United States from Sicily. He seems to have been the only malcontent. The Tallos that stayed in Sicily did very well. My Grandfather migrated to the United States in 1920. He started a dry goods company. He went door to door delivering linens. He made quite a good living.

Almost immediately after establishing himself, he married a woman named Petrina Polizzi. She was from a respected family from South Scranton. They bought a house on Pittston Avenue. After a few years of marriage, he realized his wife was not giving him an heir.

I don't know if it was frustration or male ego, but he started having an affair. It was with an Irish woman from Minooka. Unfortunately for her, she did become pregnant. At that time one of the only solutions was to put the child in an orphanage, Saint Joseph's orphanage in this case.

It would have been a great scandal to keep the baby. First, because the father was an Italian and secondly because he was married. She later married a doctor and had two children.

As my father tells the story, when he was four years old, his father then adopted him as his own. He named him Matteo and brought him home to his wife Petrina. She was not too happy. In one of my father's drunken monologues, he told me how verbally abusive she was.

He was taught Italian by his father and spoke it fluently. One of the things she would say often was, "  andare a puttana chi ti ha cagato". Remember, he knew Italian and the Sicilian dialect. He understood she was telling him to go back to the person that had birthed him, complete with profanities and intensity.

My grandmother Petrina died in 1954. Although, I don't remember her, I find it curious that she also was not an alternative to our stay at St. Josephs in 1953.

Scranton was a big industrial booming metropolis at one time. Dad would tell us how he went to work in the mines when he was 8 years old. He was a canary boy. They used canaries in coal mines to detect carbon monoxide and other toxic gases before they went into the mines. If the canary became ill or died, that would give miners a warning not to enter or to evacuate if they were already inside.

They also used children to go in first and open the trap doors that let in air. That's why they were called the Canary boys.

When Dad got a little older, he made a shoeshine box. He would visit saloons and ask if anyone wanted a shoeshine. At sixteen, he started working at the Gold Star Pants factory and that's where he met my mother, Antonette. He joined the U.S. Navy, but received a compassionate discharge after nine months citing family illness. He and my mother married in January 1948.

Lucky for him a new factory, Capitol Records pressing plant hired him. He worked nights starting at 3:30 PM. My mother worked days until 4:30 PM and got home before 5.

From age 10, I was the babysitter between 3 and 5 PM. I oversaw my younger siblings. By then there was baby Ann, Matt 5 years old and Joe 9 years old.

My father was the daytime parent. If there was an emergency with one of us that's who would come. I was about 7 years old and my brother Joe 8. We were playing 'Tag' at recess in the James Monroe Elementary School yard. I am sure it was an accident, but Joe tripped me and I hit my head on the concrete wall right by my left eyebrow. I was bleeding profusely.

When my father got there, he scooped me up and carried me to our family Doctor, Dr. Spaletta. The office was about 2 blocks away. The doctor stitched me up right there. I have a small scar at the edge of my left eyebrow. That scar reminds me that my father could be a caring parent.

For some reason my father would not let us get a dog. My brother Joe would beg and promise to take care of it to no avail. My father liked uncommon and exotic pets. We had goats and chickens in our garage. The goats did not like my brother Matthew. They would take every opportunity to butt him when he was playing in the yard. I learned how to milk a goat but I would not drink the goat's milk.

My father brought home a male Capuchin monkey and

named him George. These are the little ones you see on the organ grinder's shoulder. Due to their energetic nature, they require an active lifestyle. George would be in his cage for hours at a time.

My brothers hated him and teased him when my dad was not around. George got angry quickly and could hold a grudge. When he would be let out of the cage, he would be aggressive. He would go straight for Joe and Matt and they would run. I tried to stay in my room when he was let out of the cage. He would climb the drapes and relieve himself at will. George bit my father at least five times. Finally, my father donated him to the Nay Aug Park Zoo. We were not sorry to see him go.

When Joe was about 10, he found and brought home a miniature collie. We named her Lucky. At first it seemed that my father was ok with the dog. One day he abruptly gave Lucky away to our neighbor. Unfortunately these neighbors mistreated him. After a few weeks, Lucky dissa-peared from our neighbors porch . We had no clue what happened to him. It was heartbreaking.

Two years later, Joe and I were playing a game in the basement and we heard scratching at the back door. When we investigated, there was Lucky. If dogs could talk; she would have quite a story. Even my father was blown away at Lucky's baffling homecoming. We kept her until she died six years later.

When I was about 15, I remember the morning he came home from working the night shift at Capitol and gave me a 45-rpm vinyl record of "I Want to Hold Your Hand" by the Beatles. That was one of very few fond memories of my chaotic childhood.

I don't know when it started, but we were made to endure "Chinese Fire Drills" quite often. "Chinese fire drill" is a slang term for a situation that is chaotic or confusing, possibly due to poor or misunderstood instructions. Today, this term is considered offensive.

Hours after we fell asleep, we would awaken to our father screaming our names. Rubbing the sleep from our eyes, we would stumble down the stairs. He would have us line up and begin the interrogation. It might be about something he found broken or missing. He would berate us until one of us broke. I suspect my brother Joe confessed even when innocent just to stop the interrogation.

My parents were very strict. A decision I found unreasonable had to do with the Catholic Daughters at my church. As I said school, the library and the church were my safe havens. Catholic Daughters was the alternative version to the {Protestant} Girl Scouts. I loved being part of a group. We put on musicals and minstrels shows for the congregation.

The minstrel show portrayed the Interlocutors as black men. Two older girls in blackface. I had no idea at the time how racist this was.

Every summer the Catholic Daughters of St Johns Church held a sleepover camp. It was held at The Little Flower Camp in Tobyhanna, near the Poconos. I begged and begged to go with my peers to no avail.

I was not ever allowed to do sleepovers at any of my friends' homes. Finally, when I was 15, they let me stay at my friend Paula's house. She was Italian and Catholic so she passed the test. I didn't tell them her parents were gone away. Paula didn't tell me that her boyfriend Slick was staying over. That night I "heard" them having sex. I laid in the bed in the next room auditing Sex Education 101.

My father had to meet every boy I went out with. That was a challenging situation. Not just for the boys, but for the embarrassment it brought me. At that time, the early sixties, there were dances held every Friday. Community approved places to stay out of trouble. Mechanics Hall,

Workingman's Hall, St. Mary's, etc. Usually just playing popular records. Sometimes there was a live band.

One of my nightmare memories was when I needed a boy to meet my dad before we could go to the dance. At the time my father was making his own beer, we had a bathroom on first floor and one on the second floor. He took over the claw foot bathtub on the second floor for his brewery.

The first time I had a date with a boy, my father insisted on showing him the two dozen bottles of beer fermenting in the tub upstairs. After that I would just say I was going to one of the dances with my girlfriends.

**" A happy childhood is the worst possible preparation for life." Kinky Friedman**

# CHAPTER 3

# MUSTARD BATHS

In my next session with Dr. Lemon, he addressed that I had said very little about my mother. I didn't realize that so I proceeded to tell him about my mother's background. My mothers' parents came from the area of Bari in Italy. I was able to visit there later in my life. The town was called Alberobello, beautiful trees in English.

Her father Dominic was 15 years older than her mother Anna. He literally picked my grandmother like a flower from a garden. Of the two daughters of the Galiani family, my grandmother was the prettiest.

Dominic Copertino opened a bar and the family lived upstairs. My mother was first born like me and named Vita Antonia. For some unknown reason, they later changed her name to Antonette. They were not affectionate to their children or each other. My grandfather told my mother she should become a nun because she was not pretty enough to attract a husband.

I guess you repeat some version of what you grew up with. My mother was cold, introverted and detached. I have no memories of her ever hugging or kissing any of us. My brother Joe said she would tie him up in the basement and hit him with a garden hose. She told him her life would be much better if he had not been born.

She would work all day in the Gold Star Pants factory and come home after my father had left for the night shift at Capitol Records. It is a mystery to me how they found time to conceive four children.

I neither have good or bad memories of my mother from when I was a child. I have read that a mother's role is that of a mirror, reflecting who the daughter is. Her strengths, talents, fears, and her hopes for the future. As a result of not having a maternal mirror, I grew up feeling unseen and misunderstood. I suffered from low self-esteem and a high degree of self-doubt.

I learned housekeeping skills from my father. He was the one who taught me how to fold laundry, make a bed with hospital corners and cook. He was the one that helped me with homework when I was in elementary school. He was the one that handled all my medical emergencies. Maybe that is another reason why I never developed a bond with my mother.

Later in life I had to place my mother in a nursing home. I picked what I thought was the best one in the area, The Jewish Home. I had worked there when I was in high school. I knew it was clean, the food was good and they took good care of their patients.

My mother was very angry at me for placing her there. However, she could not take care of herself or her apartment. She was becoming a hoarder and keeping old newspapers and junk mail in trash bags. She was also a compulsive shopper and ordering daily from QVC.

Her sister Jane was in the same facility so that made it a little more agreeable.

I was living in Florida at the time, so I got her a cell phone. When I brought her the cell phone, she said, "Why are you so nice to me?" I replied:" Because you're my mother."

I also gave her a journal called: "Mom, Tell Me Your Story, a guided journal". I thought that would be a nice thing for me to have after she died. After she passed, I took the little book back to Florida with me. She didn't have entries under many of the sections, but there was one entry that clearly explained our lack of a bond.

Under the heading," Starting A Family: How did you feel when you found out you were going to be a mom?"

She wrote " When I realized I was pregnant, I jumped up and down the hallway steps multiple times, and took mustard baths every day to end it. But it didn't work".

***Love the heart that hurts you,***
***but never hurt the heart that loves you.***
***- Vipin Sharma***

# CHAPTER 4

# CHILD LABOR

Scranton was a big drinking town. During the coal boom in the 1800's Anthracite was first quarried from outcrops. When quarrying became impractical, the miners went underground. The coal miners would work a 12-hour day. Covered in soot they would stop at the bar before they went home. Drinking had been just what the hardworking men did. Work hard drink hard!

There was a bar on every corner. They would drink in their neighborhood bar and then stumble home. No fear of a DUI, then. Even after the mines closed that mentality continued in our valley. There were only two kinds of drinkers in my hometown. Those that were in the bar drinking and those that were in AA meetings. The popular opinion was that the drunks in AA couldn't hold their liquor. Getting drunk wasn't seen as a bad thing. However, public drunkenness was frowned upon. It was acting drunk that brought shame. I had an alcoholic father that often embarrassed me in front of my friends and was the bane of my life.

When I was about 15, a roller-skating rink opened called Town Hall. My friends and I were so excited. I didn't even know how to roller skate, but I learned fast. After all, that's where the boys were. We would all skate round and round the rink in a circle. The hardest part to learn was how to make the turns. Popular music of the day was played such as The Beachboys, Leslie Gore, Dion, etc.

One Saturday I was skating and trying not to let the boys see me looking at them. Out of the corner of my eye who did I see but my father. Of course, he was drunk. I watched with horror as he rented a pair of skates. He got into the rink and he started to skate. I pretended I didn't know who he was.

He didn't get very far before he crashed into the guard-rails and fell. He couldn't get up. People came over to help him and they had to call an ambulance. It turns out he broke his wrist. I was happy that happened. He didn't come back again. The Gods had let me keep at least one place of my own. Here I was with a drunken father, who made beer in the bathtub and it seemed like there was no escape from this hell.

My dream was to be a High School English teacher. I was

a voracious reader. I grew up right across the street from a library. I had a branch of the public library right across the street and our church a block away. These were very good places for me to escape to. They were places that my parents would not declare off limits. I would go to that library and check out a bunch of books. Run upstairs to my room. Put the Platters or Temptations on the record player and I'd be up there for hours.

One time my father came to the door and said I was spending too much time in my room and demanded I come down with the rest of the family. So, I started going downstairs and watching TV at night with the family.

I loved school and I was so blessed to have had a wonderful English teacher in seventh grade. Mrs. Wilder would not only tell you about the book, she would act it out. Then she would assign parts to some of us in class and do a little play. I fell in love with her. She stoked the fire of my love of reading.

She had talked about a book called "Gone with the Wind." I wanted to get that book as soon as I got home from school that day. The library had a children's section and an adult section. I was only 14 or 15th time. This book was in the adult section and the librarian would not let me check it out.

So back across the street I went and asked my mother to please check this book out for me. I told her the teacher told me to read it. My mother did go over and checked it out.

When first published, Margaret Mitchell's Gone with the Wind was banned on social grounds. The book had been called "offensive" and "vulgar" because of the language and characterizations. Words like "damn" and "whore" were scandalous at the time. The New York Society for the Suppression of Vice disapproved of Scarlett's multiple marriages. The term used to describe slaves was also offensive to some readers. In time the membership of the lead characters in the Ku Klux Klan became problematic.

Being a teenager, I was more focused on the love triangle. I was an A student and my love of reading had me placed in an AP English class. I still had the dream of going to college.

My parents instilled in me and my brother Joe that we had to work to get things that were not necessities. We had jobs after school from about 9 to 10 years of age. As a teenager , I had to pay for the dentist and buy my own clothes.

I cleaned Mrs. Frank's 5 & 10 store and walked down the hill every night to pick up her dinner at Smith's Restaurant.

Joe shined shoes in bars at night and did other odd jobs.

When I was almost 16 and Joe 15, we both got jobs working at a bakery for Sam Miller. Five days a week after school. My job was wrapping the bread and other baked goods. There was a hot griddle type plate. I would wrap the cellophane around the product and then place it momentarily on the hot griddle to seal it. I got quite a few burns. My brother helped the bakers. Getting supplies out of the storage room etc.

One of the bakers was a stunning man named Steve Mellin. He was in his late twenties, was married and had children. He flirted with me all the time. I loved the attention.

I still had not learned to drive. That was the ruse that got me to be alone with him. Steve offered to help me learn, I still had homework waiting at home, but I would go with him for a short while. He would find a deserted lot or sometimes drive to Nay Aug Park. The driving lessons turned out to be make out sessions. I had never kissed a man before, just boys. There was no comparison.

After a few weeks, he started to tell me he was in love with me. He wanted us to run away together. I was torn between the headrush of this man telling me he loved me and my Catholic upbringing . So, I did what any good Catholic girl would do. I went to confession.

I told the priest I was having an affair with a married man. He told me to put myself in the wife's shoes. As soon as he said that, I knew what I had to do. The next night when I went for "my driving lesson", I broke it off with Steve.

The ironic part was that my brother Joe had followed us that night. He saw me with Steve. My brother had me on a pedestal since the bond we formed in the orphanage. That night, I fell off that pedestal. At home, he confronted me and told me how disappointed he was in me. I was no longer the saint, he thought I was.

For years I romanticized that fling with Steve. Finally, I realized that legally he would be labeled a pedophile. The priest never mentioned that the actions of this married 25-year-old man were sinful and inappropriate. No, he put the blame and shame on me.

I will not judge Steve for the short-lived affair. But I have changed the lens through which I see this experience. I no longer perceive it as a May-December romance. I now see it for what it was. An adult man preying on a naive girl.

**The universe gives us unlimited opportunities and unlimited messengers. There was a pattern emerging. A pattern I wouldn't see for many years.**

# CHAPTER 5

# INNOCENCE LOST

In 1965 Inspired by John Kennedy, James Walsh ran for mayor of Scranton, challenging the Democratic Party structure and the party's endorsed candidate, Jim McGee. I was asked to be a "Walsh Girl". A group of young girls that would go to rallies and ride in convertibles in parades. I was just 16. We had red and white outfits with capes. Basically, eye candy.

One night at a rally, one of the older guys working for the candidate asked me to help him. We were at the Hotel Casey. He took me upstairs to one of the suites to get more beverages for the party downstairs. I should have realized something was wrong, when he didn't turn on the lights. Before I knew it, he picked me up and started to carry me towards the bed. I was able to get away and ran downstairs. Marty was about 30 years old. I was more aware of my surroundings after that. Sexual inappropriateness was not really addressed then. I felt ashamed. I never told anyone.

I was starting to realize that men like that are attracted to girls who they think are easy to manipulate and control.

My senior year I was looking forward to going to college. In 1966 we had two big colleges in Scranton. Marywood College, which was for girls and the University of Scranton which was for boys. I graduated in a high school class of 500 students. We had a huge senior class. The Scranton Central High School was a college prep school. Most students were planning on going to college.

After the graduation ceremony my parents gave me a watch as a graduation present. Then they informed me that they would not be able to support me going to college. Their belief was that the college was wasted on girls because ultimately, they were going to get married and have children. They said I needed to stay home and get a job and help the family. I was crushed. I was 17 years old and my brain and my temperament, personality and resourcefulness was not adequate enough to defend my dream. I did not have the courage or capability to figure out a way to go anyway without their permission. It seemed like an insurmountable problem.

I was dating a boy that was a year younger than me at the time. I had met him at a dance and he did not go to our school so I didn't know how old he was when I met him. Curt was a sweetheart. He really fell head over heels in love with me. I started dating him in March. By June my feelings had simmered down. However, I needed a date for the prom. I wasn't going to break up with him until after my Senior Prom.

I went to the prom with the explicit plan of losing my virginity that night.

I wore this full-length dress with a yellow bodice and enormous skirt embroidered with daisies. In spite of the size of the dress, I fulfilled my mission. In the back seat of his 1964 Mustang. Oh, the flexibility of youth.

That summer Curt became an annoyance. I just didn't care for him and it got so bad that when he kissed me, I would literally want to throw up. By Midsummer I had broken it off with Curt. He was very upset about it.

One night I was coming home from a dance and he was literally waiting for me in the dark. He scared the shit out of me. He got on his knees and begged for me to take him back. I can't believe I did this but I actually said "You are not much of a man if you're on your knees. "

I went to a dance a couple weeks later at Workingman's Hall. During intermission this gorgeous blonde boy walked up to me. He looked like James Caan in the 60's. The way Caan looked in the Godfather, when he played Sonny Corleone. Curly blonde hair and green eyes.

We started talking and he told me he was leaving to go in the Navy the next day. He asked if I would write to him. Of course, I said yes... he wrote down his military address on a matchbook cover and I promised I would write to him. That promise changed my life in ways I could not imagine.

# CHAPTER 6

# CAPITOL GIRLS

After graduation, mother got me a job in the Gold Star pants factory with her. That was the worst summer of my life. I had two Italian ladies, one on each side of me. They would talk all day, telling dirty jokes and using filthy language. My face would just be red the whole day. One of them, Sofia, said to me," honey, you don't belong here, you belong in an office".

By the end of the summer, I did find a job in an office, Capitol Records. Not the plant where my father worked, but the record club company.  Back then companies like Columbia Records and Capitol Records had subscription clubs. The customer would sign up and every month he would get the record of the month. My position there was in customer service. I loved my job.

At Capitol Records I met people that I would be friends with for decades, Janet, Pat, Priscilla, and Marlene. We were all young, dating and looking forward to getting married someday and having children. We would get together once a week, alternating at each other's homes.

We shared everything, our joys, and our heartbreaks. Janet first had her heart broken by a handsome Italian attorney she was dating. Then she met a State Trooper that is still her husband today. They have been married for probably 40 years or more.

Priscilla was our favorite. We loved her so much. She was very funny and so beautiful. She looked like Elizabeth Taylor but with blonde hair. She was very self-conscious about her weight even though none of us cared about her size. She was crazy about this guy, who worked for the Scranton Times. He was a very passive guy, but for some reason is nickname was Killer. She practically stalked him. He finally had to give in and they got married. They had two children, Dayna, and Bryan.

Annmarie was going with a very good-looking Italian boy from Old Forge. They seemed very much in love. They got married young and had a son. However, it turned out he was not capable of fidelity. She got divorced and never remarried.

Pat was in love with a man who owned a million-dollar business and was very well known. They went out for years, however he was not interested in marriage. He broke her heart. To this day she has never married.

I worked at Capitol records for a couple years and I met some famous people. One day The Righteous Brothers came in, Bobby Hatfield and Bill Medley. I remember noting that Bobby was very nice and friendly. However, Bill Medley was a little bit of a snob and uppity. Then we got the news that Capitol was closing the record club division in Scranton. They were building a beautiful new building in Los Angeles.

They asked the top employees; the most productive people go to Los Angeles and train people. I thought this was it. This is my escape. The company was going to pay for my plane ticket. They had a building with apartments for just the Capitol employees. My friend Marlene was going to go. This was great because I would not have to be alone in a strange city.

I went home so excited that night and told my parents all about it. My father started to yell at me. “He said if you try to leave and go to California I will jump in front of the airplane.” There's no way he was going to let me leave.

When I look back on it, I think why didn’t I pack secretly and run away in the middle of the night. I could have stayed at my friend Marlene's house.

I could have boarded the plane the next day. I guess my training had always been to be meek and subservient to adults. My self-confidence was too fragile to stand up for myself.

Another getaway plan thwarted!

# CHAPTER 7

# SOLDIER BOYS

It was 1967 the Vietnam War was still going on. I knew a lot boys that had been drafted. I was writing Jack Calvey who had joined the Navy. It was the judge's idea not his. At that time, when young men were arrested for non-felonies, the judge would give them a choice. Jail or the Military. Most of them chose the military.

That winter of 67, we had more than the usual amount of snow. This particular day I was shoveling the front sidewalk. A boy I never saw before came up to me, grabbed the extra shovel that was leaning against the fence and started shoveling. I asked him why he was doing that. He said, "You look like you could use some help, cutie".

That's how I met Jimmy Carr. It's interesting that like my random meeting with Jack Calvey, he was also leaving the next day for the military, the Marines. When we shoveled the front sidewalk, he also asked me to write to him. I said I would. I guess this was my way of contributing to the war effort, writing to these guys. The thing about writing to servicemen, especially during wartime, it can get intimate quickly. That's what had already happened with Jack.

I was on the bus one day going downtown and I saw a few girls that I knew from high school. I told them about Jack and that I was writing to him. One of the girls told me you're not the only one. It seems he had been writing to a few girls. One of the girls I knew very well. Her name was Betty.

I called her and asked "are you writing Jack?" She said "yes, I am". I made a date to meet with her. We both brought our letters. The son of a bitch was practically writing the same thing to both of us. I continued to write to Jack, but I let him know that I knew about the other girls. I realized he wasn't as committed as I was. So, I started dating and going out with my friends.

After a few months, I found myself getting enamored with both Jimmy and Jack. These boys were poles apart. Jimmy went to Vietnam. Jack ended up in Iceland. The songs from that time were about soldiers away at war. There was a song called Jimmy Mack.

**"Oh, Jimmy Mack when are you comin' back**

**Oh, Jimmy Mack when are you comin' back**

**My arms are missing you,**

**My lips feel the same way too**

**I tried so hard to be true, like I promised to do**

**But this guy keeps comin' around**

**He's tryin' to wear my resistance down**

**"Jimmy Mack when are you coming back**

There were also a lot of serious songs, protest songs about the Vietnam War and the toll it was having on our soldiers. The Unknown Soldier was written and recorded by The Doors and released in early 1968. It recalls the death of a faceless soldier in combat, while life goes on at home ("news is read" and "children fed").

When Jimmy came back from Vietnam, he came to see me at my house late at night. He looked very gaunt and sad. Gone was the sparkling personality of the boy who shoveled my sidewalk. We talked. He told me how much my letters meant to him. He said they were the only thing that kept him going. We made out some, second base.

I gave him an 8 x 10 picture of me. He left that night and I never saw him again. About two weeks after that, his obituary was in the Scranton Times newspaper. He had committed suicide. I was stunned and devastated to my core.

While the majority of Vietnam Veterans successfully readjusted to postwar life, a substantial number of Vietnam-era Veterans had suffered from a variety of psychological problems, and had experienced a wide range of life-adjustment problems.

Who knows what horrors Jimmy C. saw over there?

# CHAPTER 8

# JEOPARDY

One night I went to a bar downtown with my friend Arlene. Neither one of us was 21. But we both had a fake ID. I still remember my fake name. It was Beverly Colangelo and she was 28. I looked about 15. We went to this place called the Cheetah lounge. The doorman barely glanced at my fake ID. I had one drink. I wasn't a drinker back then.

Around midnight Arlene and I left and began to walk home. It was very common at that time to walk everywhere. A boy I knew named Billy Cerra asked if he could walk us home. I said we're good, we don't need you to do that. I knew he had gone on a few dates with another friend of mine, Carol. But I didn't know him well. He was from the other side of town.

He insisted that he walk us home. We got to Arlene's house first. I said Goodnight to her. My house was maybe four more blocks. When we got to Brook Street, which was a very steep hill, he said, "Oh, let's run down this hill. It will be fun." He grabbed my hand and next thing I knew we're running down the hill. You can't stop running once you start, it's just that steep of a hill. He held my hand tightly. When we got to the end of the hill, there was an alley that went behind my house. I'm not going to go back up that steep hill, so we turned into the alley.

As soon as we entered that alley, he punched me in the face. There were rocks on the ground. He picked one up and held it over my head. He said scream and I will kill you. I have never been so terrified in my life.

Somehow, I had the presence of mind to say, "My Dad's garage is right in the middle of the alley. Why don't we just go inside the garage instead of doing this outside"?

He pulled me up and we began to walk towards my garage. He still had the rock in his hand. Suddenly he stopped and said, "You are trying to trick me." My basic instincts just took over.

Suddenly everything went black and I was screaming. It just occurred organically. I didn't tell myself to scream. I just started to scream. The neighbors put their heads out the window and two of them came outside. These two men started to chase him. Unfortunately, they did not catch him. Mercifully, I was not raped. It still was a very traumatic night.

My father insisted that I call the police. I didn't want to. I was pushed to go through the whole process. The nightmare of testifying to the grand jury. It didn't even make it to court. I had two witnesses that saw him running away but they couldn't be sure who he was. Even though I knew his name. He denied it was him.

Years later I ran into him in The Globe Department Store. He walked up to me as if we were buddies and he said hello. I said "Don't you know who I am?" You could see the light come into his eyes as he remembered. I guess I was one of many. Since I was in his presence, I decided to ask him how did he get away with it.

He looked at me and said, very matter of fact, "Well, it cost my parents a lot of money." I took that to mean that somebody got bought off. I guess the DA. Later, Karma got him because he got arrested several times for rape and attempted rape. Although they never seemed to be able to convict him of rape charges. Eventually he was convicted of robbery and sent to jail for few years.

The rape attempt was very traumatic. I spent days in bed incredibly depressed. Jack's mother came to see me and gave me a pep talk. She motivated me to get out of bed and on with my life.

Around the same time my father and my brother Joe went to Reedman's in Lancaster to buy a new car. They came home with a 1969 Black Thunderbird. As soon as my mother saw it, she pulled my father aside. She told him that this was not an appropriate car for our family.

I offered to buy it from my dad. He agreed to let me give him monthly payments. That car really cheered me up and it attracted the boys. I couldn't wait till that Friday to drive to Papa Joes in Archibald. Of course, the boys all went crazy. They asked me to take them for a ride.

When we got on Route 81, I sped up. I don't know what got into me, but I started to go faster and faster. When I finally looked at the speedometer, it read 100 mph. Looking back, I think it made me feel powerful, a feeling I had never experienced before.

A few days later, my father took the Thunderbird to run some errands. When he returned, he told me our deal was off. That car was too fast for a young girl like me, I was furious at the time. Now I thank God because I know he was right.

**"She'll have fun, fun, fun until Daddy takes the T-Bird away"  The Beachboys**

# CHAPTER 9

# THE GREAT ESCAPE

Jack came to see me when he was on leave. He seemed devastated that I had gone through such trauma. He felt bad that he wasn't there for me. He was so charming and the chemistry was off the charts. After he returned to the ship we continued to write. The letters got steamy. When he got discharged from the Navy, he called me. We went to the movies and had a nice evening.

On the way home there was this telephone pole with a wooden box on the side. Who knows why that box was there? Jack turned into an opportunity for a very romantic moment. He turned over that crate and picked me up and put me on top of it. It was as if he was putting me on a pedestal. He looked at me with those beautiful green eyes and proposed.

So here I was offered another escape route. I did love him. I was very into him, but if I had a nicer home environment, I probably would have waited a little longer to get married.

The next night he insisted on asking my father for my hand in marriage. My father was drinking and did not take the proposal well. First, he took me in another room and proceeded to tell me that Jack just wanted to get in my pants. After an unbelievably long time with him postulating on the devious ways of young men, he gave up that line of attack. He realized he just wasn't going to sway me.

He then proceeded to take Jack down into the basement to talk to him. Later, Jack told me that my father said I didn't love him and the only reason I said yes was, so I could get out of my house and be free from my family. There was more than a grain of truth in that. At this point Jack had enough. He went to the front door, looked at me sadly and left. I looked at my mother. There was nothing in her eyes to influence me. I picked up my purse and I went out the door. That night I stayed at my grandmother's.

I did not return home. Jack and I were married a few weeks later. At that time, you had to be 21 to get married. You had to be 21 to vote and to drink. I was 19 and going to be 20 in a month. I had to ask my mother to sign for me at the courthouse for the marriage license. She did.

We had a church wedding in the church I grew up in, St.

John's the Evangelist. My parents had a small party at the house. I still have a few pictures of the day. I looked happy and Jack looked confused.

They say you marry your father. He was just a younger cuter version of my father. I went from the frying pan into the fire.

At first, we had our honeymoon period and everything seemed wonderful. After a few weeks I started noticing things. The fact that he hadn't gotten a job. He wanted to be with me all the time. I had gotten a great job at Aetna insurance as an underwriter.

He hated when I left for work, but someone had to pay the bills.

# CHAPTER 10

# CAGED BIRD

One night we had my cousin Annamae came over for dinner. He invited his cousin Larry. I guess we were doing a little matchmaking. There was some drinking after dinner. Jack put romantic music on our record player. Larry began to kiss Annamae. At some point the inference was made that we should switch. My cousin walked out of our apartment in a huff.

I too was very upset so I don't blame her. I told Larry to go home and had a terrible blow up with Jack. I didn't understand how after three months of marriage he thought we should get into swinging or kinky stuff like that.

I wanted to believe he was my soulmate in all areas. There was a pattern emerging. One which would take me decades to realize. In looking for freedom, I had walked into a physical, sexual, and emotional prison.

I had married Jack in 1968. The character defects I had avoided looking at before started to emerge. He would get drunk every weekend. He could not seem to find a job. He was very controlling and possessive. Very early into the marriage, I suspected he was fooling around.

He would talk me into taking the day off from work to be with him. I was young and naïve. I did not realize that after a certain amount of "sick days", I could be fired. I got called into the office one day and told I had taken more than four sick days in the last two months. I was fired. I was so upset. I loved that job.

Jack was trying to get help from the V.A. to pursue a career in drafting. Meanwhile, he was not bringing any money into the household. He just sat around and drank. I had to go back to work at the dreaded Gold Star factory.

This was the first apartment for both of us and the first time we lived apart from any authority but ourselves. We had a skylight in the living room ceiling and I would love it when it rained. I would lie on the floor looking up at the rain filled sky. Imagining I was a bird flying above the clouds, free.

It was a small apartment, but charming. Our landlord, however, was crazy. I was running a bath one day and he came up the stairs, went into the bathroom and shut off the water. He told me I was using too much water. Jack almost threw him down the stairs.

Not long after that, Jack was drunk and arguing with the landlord about something. This time he put his fist through the front door glass. That was the first time we had to move. I thought "OK" we will  just treat this as a fresh start.

We moved into a first-floor apartment over a bar. The bar Morgan's was in the basement. I wasn't allowed to go into a bar without Jack. One day I decided to go down to pay the rent. I came out of the basement bar and started to go into our apartment. Jack was pulling up at the same moment. He started screaming and pulling my hair. I was determined not to have him get me inside the house. I held onto the railing for dear life. Finally, the police came and told him to cool off, take it easy.

We had to move again. My mother had a friend who had a second-floor apartment. She lived downstairs and we lived upstairs. She heard all the noise and fights and everything that went on. Of course, she reported it all to my mom.

My brother Joe was getting married. The family was having a bridal shower for his fiancé Barb. She was picking me up in her car. Jack did not want me to go. He never wanted me to be around family or friends. I knew it wasn't normal but I didn't realize how abusive it was. I was young and unsophisticated. That day I realized how abusive he could be.

When Barbara beeped the horn, I was unable to come out of the apartment. He literally had tied me to the kitchen chair. He told her I was tied up and couldn't attend the shower. If that was his attempt at humor, it was very sick humor. He then untied me and was lovey dovey the rest of the day.

After that it got even worse. He never hit me, hair pulling and pinching were his forte. A month of abuse went by before I fled to my parents' home. After I left, he sold all of our furniture and all our belongings.

In those days' girls started a Hope Chest before they got married. I had saved green stamps for years to collect a full set of beautiful silver and white china. Some of you might not know what green stamps are. Green Stamps were one of the first retail loyalty programs, by which retailers purchased the stamps from the Sperry & Hutchinson company and then gave them away at a rate determined by the merchant. Some shoppers would choose one merchant over another because they gave out more stamps per dollar spent Certain grocery stores, gas stations and department stores gave you stamps when you bought things and you saved them in a book. When you had enough books, you could redeem them for merchandise.

I had acquired enough books for a beautiful silver and white china set. He sold the dishes that I had saved up for so long. Jack knew how special that set of china was. He knew how upset I was that it was gone. Yet he kept pursuing me and asking me for forgiveness.

His charming ways, his handsome face, the chemistry, everything finally wore me down. I forgave him and believed his promise to never mistreat me again. We now had literally nothing and so moved into a furnished apartment. He started taking drafting courses under the VA program. He was still drinking and verbally abusing me. Then he'd want to kiss and make love. Sexually he was more than competent. If I had a top ten, he would be number 2 on the list. Sex was so good that all would be forgiven.

I was still working in the sweatshop. I was getting more and more depressed. I guess it was obvious to everyone around me at the factory. A co-worker told me that I probably could get workmen's compensation. She had done it a year ago, citing a mental breakdown. Because I was truly very depressed, I filed for it. I got the approval, but it took weeks before I would get the first check. That first check would be the big one. So, I was holding on to my sanity and dignity by my fingertips.

One night I was in such a sorry state that I took a handful of tranquilizers. I called my friend Annmarie, who was studying to be a nurse. She told me to immediately put my finger down my throat and throw up. After I did that, I realized how mentally unwell I was. As soon as that check came in, I left. I remember taking my wedding band off and leaving it on the kitchen table for him. No note just the ring.

I rented a room in the Carter Apartments for Women. Men were not allowed in the building. One day Jack came into the building and up the stairs to the apartment I was staying in. He knocked on the door and again begged for forgiveness. I stood fast. I had never lived alone. I was very lonely. I sent him away, determined to face my fears.

At night I would experience intense anxiety. I was incapable of being alone. I would just have such apprehension. I started going to a bar called O'Tooles to get through the night. It was near the University of Scranton campus. I would go there and have a drink. Inevitably a guy would buy me a drink or two. By the time I went home, I was sufficiently buzzed to go to sleep. That was my solution at the moment.

One night I met a guy that used to be a neighbor when I was growing up in South Side. James B. was a little older than me. He sat down in the booth and we had a drink. Suddenly I looked up and there was Jack and his mother, Dorothy.

She was an aggressive, intimidating woman. She could scare the shit out of anybody. They came over to the booth where I sat with James. Dorothy started to berate me and call me a whore and a slut. Shouting that I was a married woman and here I am in a bar with another man.

James knew me since we were kids. He knew I was none of those things. He just sat there calmly and smiled. Unable to rattle us they finally gave up and left.

That night was the first time I had sex outside of my marriage to Jack. Afterwards, I said to James, "am I going to hell? " He laughed and said not for having sex. He really made me feel better that night.

Ironically, I ended up getting a job at O'Tooles as a cocktail waitress. That summer I never felt lonely again. It was 1970, The Summer of Love. Everyone just wanted to get high. Make love not war.

The marriage to Jack had been a futile attempt to break the cycle of feeling powerless. I filed for divorce.

# CHAPTER 11

# PETTY TYRANTS

The seventies turned out to be a trend-laden, fad-crazy decade. We all listened to 8-track tapes of Jackson Browne, Olivia Newton-John, and Marvin Gaye. Disco was born, the sounds of Abba, the Bee Gees and Donna Summer. Every party you went to would have cheese fondue. This was the decade of wife-swapping parties and smoking pot. I guess Jack was ahead of his time with the wife-swapping attempt.

People were wearing what they wanted, growing their hair long, having sex, doing drugs. For the first time in my life, I was totally free to do as I liked. I smoked pot and liked it. No, I loved it. Sex didn't mean love so there was a lot of that.

One day, another Jim walked into my life. I was working at O'Tooles. Jim Brazil watched me whizzing around serving drinks for about an hour. He then called me over to his booth and asked me if I wanted a job. I said I already had a job. He wanted me to waitress at a new place on Moosic

Street called, The Upstairs. It was run by Benny Santoro and Billy Schreiber.

I took the job and made more money right away. Grown men tipped better than college students. Billy Schreiber was a bit of a tyrant. You could never please him. Benny Santoro on the other hand was a doll. I didn't know at the time if Benny's family was "connected'. There was a big crime family presence in Scranton.

The Buffalino crime family, was an Italian-American Mafia crime family active in Northeastern Pennsylvania, primarily in the cities of Scranton, Wilkes-Barre, and Pittston. The Don lived in Pittston and was connected to the "Five Families". The organization spanned from Philadelphia to Los Angles. Benny's father Vito was rumored to be one the Buffalino family's trusted soldiers.

The Upstairs was primarily a forum for dancing and Rock music. It was ear splitting loud and hard to hear the drink orders. Billy did not miss my unmistaken ability as a cocktail waitress. He had more of a stake in the bar downstairs, simply called the Downstairs at the Upstairs. This was more of a laid-back lounge. He wanted me to work there. That meant he was now supervising me, not laid-back Benny.

I remember one night the place was packed and I was the only waitress. Every time I walked by him, he would say, "Hustle, Hustle, Hustle." He really got under my skin. I was his best waitress, but he would never tell me that.

There was a band that played upstairs that had an organist who was partly deaf. I thought that was amazing that he was able to be a musician despite his disability. The Downstairs closed earlier than the Upstairs. After I finished work, I would go Upstairs for a drink. One night the band had me on stage with them. I couldn't sing or play an instrument, so they gave me a tambourine. I had such fun that night.

Frankie, the organist, and I were very attracted to each other. We ended up at his apartment a few times. All I can say about sex with him was that it was quite acrobatic.

I called him one night, a booty call to be honest. I had been drinking, but drove to his place in Dupont. I made a left turn that was too wide and almost hit another car. There was yelling and cursing. I did not get out of the car. There was not actually an accident, so I drove off. I still did not realize at the time that I had a problem with alcohol.

Fourth of July that year, I had the day off. I made plans to go to a clambake with some friends. That morning, Billy

S. called and told me I had to work. When I told him, it was my day off, he could care less. He said "Come in or you're fired?" I was angered, I yelled back, "I quit" and hung up the phone. Good thing I was living with my parents again because I was now unemployed.

A few weeks later, I needed to take a cab somewhere. The cab driver looked familiar. It turned out he was a regular from The Downstairs. He told me driving a cab was just a side job. He was also the manager of a neighborhood bar called the Black Garter and could use a cocktail waitress. Unfortunately, Bill S, my former boss was the owner. He said don't worry, he never comes in. He won't even know you are on his payroll.

The next week I started my adventure at the Black Garter. That's where I met Johnny Donahue. The universe just kept sending me clones of my father. I guess that happens until you learn the lesson the Universe is trying to teach you.

# CHAPTER 12

# KISMET

The first time I saw Johnny Donahue was when I walked into my new job at the Black Garter. I was there to start as a new cocktail waitress. It was a cheesy neighborhood bar with peanut shells on the floor. That was a big thing back in the 70s.

Johnny was behind the bar having a drink, Dewar's on the rocks. He was the skinniest, whitest Irish guy I had ever seen. He had a crooked smile and straight brown hair. But the charm, the Irish charm just oozed out of his body. Right from the beginning I knew I was in trouble. He wasn't handsome but there was a roguish attractiveness to his face. A vulnerability in his eyes and a rakish smile. He was very charming and very funny. He flirted with me from the second we met.

The Black Garter was very accepting of drug culture. I was smoking pot on a regular basis as most of my friends and acquaintances were doing. I had a dealer named Kevin. I don't know if he's still alive, so I won't use his last name.

I distinctly remember his full name because of writing him a check every week for $20.00 for an ounce of marijuana. I just think that's amusing on several levels. First, that I wrote a check. I don't know what the prices are today, but $20.00 for an ounce of Columbian Gold was probably cheap. Back in the day we rolled our joints by hand. We bought papers and there was an art to rolling the perfect joint. I had very small hands so I was very good at it.

It was just understood that when you had a break at the bar you could go outside to the back parking lot and have a couple puffs on a joint. Then go back to work. One night it's very busy. On my break, I went out back with some people. We shared a joint. Johnny decided to play a joke on me that night. There was a bottle of beer in the cooler that had formed some ice on the bottom. When I went to pick up my tray of drinks for a table, he had put the drinks and that bottle of beer with the ice on my tray. Of course, the beer bottle was tilted. I didn't see the ice on the bottom. I just saw the tilted bottle. I started to get paranoid, anxious. My first thought was maybe the pot had been laced with LSD. I began to ask Johnny and people around me, "is that bottle tilted or am I seeing things? "

They were all in in on the joke. Everyone said, I don't know what you're talking about. Finally, after getting me sufficiently worked up they all started to laugh. Johnny picked up the bottle and showed me the little bit of ice on the bottom. That was the environment that I was working in, which I have to say I liked very much. Fun and games. Sex, Drugs and Rock and Roll. The Seventies!

Whenever business was slow Johnny would teach me how to make cocktails. The clink of the ice, the free pour of liquor, the shaker, it was an art form. The caveat was if I made it, then I had to drink it. I only tried to learn one or two drinks a shift. I remember so well his knowledge and skill. Then people drank very classic drinks. Yes, there were shot and beer drinkers. Yes, there were people that had scotch on the rocks or a glass of wine. However, there were also people that liked Sidecars, Old Fashioneds, Manhattan's and Martinis. I learned every one of those classic drinks from Johnny. I continued to work there a few months. Even though I was a waitress, it was like going to night school learning to be a mixologist.

Johnny and I had been sleeping together. Naturally, he had the sexual prowess to match his charm. He also had this aura of a tragic hero. I always felt that he had some heartbreak buried deep in his soul. On the outside he had the banter and the sense of humor. However, it was evident that his innermost being was fiercely guarded. He was also a rogue. I knew he was but I loved him anyway. I was spellbound.

I believe we each have a major pattern to resolve in our lifetime. A major portion of my life was spent uncovering, forgiving, resolving that pattern. I still had decades to live before I would recognize my pattern.

One day we heard there was an opening at the Hotel Casey. This iconic hotel had opened in 1911. At the time it was the largest hotel in Northeastern Pennsylvania with eleven stories and 250 rooms. Johnny and I both applied for the day bartending job.

It was considered a landmark of the city of Scranton and one of the top hotels in the Northeastern United States. I did not tell Johnny that I was going to apply for the bartender job. I was in the middle of my interview when Johnny walked in. He was there to interview for the same job. The look on his face was priceless.

Three days later the Hotel Casey called me and told me I had the job. It was a day job so that was good. But it was also boring because during the day it was slow. The Hotel Casey bar sat on the corner of Adams and Lackawanna Avenues.

There were three entrances to the bar. You could come in from a door on Adams Avenue or you could come in from Lackawanna Avenue or you could come in through the lobby. The bar was a beautiful mahogany oval shaped masterpiece. The logistics of the design meant if I was at one end of the bar and someone came in the other end of the bar, I would not see them. The result being I had to walk around the bar constantly. Round and Round, in fear that I wouldn't see a customer come in.

At one point they offered me night shift. The night shift would be busier therefore my tip income would be much larger. I met a lot of very important people. Very well-known people, famous people, odd people. I also made phenomenal tips. To sweeten the deal, they gave me a hotel room to live in. When I got off work at one or two in the morning, I could just go up in the elevator to my room.

The Hotel Casey was comparable to The Plaza Hotel in New York City. Marble staircase, Chandeliers everywhere. They had a coffee shop, a barber, a fancy restaurant. The Gold Room and Mei King Restaurant were built in the French Renaissance style. Originally it was just the Gold Room. The Chinese restaurant was added to attract more diners.

There was a bell hop named Marshall. Everyone else called him Peewee but I called him by his given name. A woman named Gina worked in the coffee shop. She became an unconventional mother figure for me. She was Vito Santoro's girlfriend. Vito was Benny and Jimmy Santoro's father.

Since the early 1900's the Hotel was known as the unofficial Democratic Headquarters. Many politicians and famous people have stayed there. Just to name a few, Orson Welles, President Nixon, Nat King Cole, Robert F. Kennedy, Jerry Lewis, and Joe DiMaggio. About 1962 the hotel started to go downhill.

In 1969 three doctors from Dunmore bought it, Frangelli, Scrimalli and Petrillo. Dr. Petrillo was Pete's Uncle. Pete Petrillo was quite a character. Downtown Scranton was a little rough back then. I felt safe with all my male friends and living in the hotel. I was making a lot of money working there. I would make $50-$100 a night in tips.

Almost all aspects of American society in the 1970s was marked by restlessness. My enjoyment of freedom for the first time in my life also led me to some bad habits. Drinking too much, overspending and a devil-may-care attitude about life in general.

Addiction often goes together with avoidance. The opposite of that avoidance would have been self-reflection. I was not ready for that. Instead, I spent too much money on status symbols like clothes, jewelry, and weed. At 23 years of age, I had no inkling that not only was a recession coming, but my income would also take a nose dive.

**"It often occurs to me that we love most what makes us miserable. In my opinion the damned are damned because they enjoy being damned."**

**Patrick Kavanagh**

# CHAPTER 13

# HINKY RELATIONSHIPS

Johnny and I continued in our relationship. He just laughed at the turn of events when I got the job at the Hotel Casey. He also got a better job than the Black Garter. Ironically, it was at the Cheetah Lounge, where I had the run-in with the would-be rapist.

He was drinking a lot more. Many bartenders tend to be alcoholics. It is the one job where you can drink booze for free and get away with it. Johnny's drink was Dewar's Scotch on the rocks. One day I got a call that they had taken him by ambulance to the hospital. He was serving a customer and then he was on the floor unconscious. Bloodwork showed severe anemia and liver problem. Not many people were using the word alcoholic then, but that's what he was. The way I was drinking put me on that road too.

The next night a beautiful black woman came in the Hotel Casey bar. Her name was Nikki. She ordered a drink, an expensive drink, Courvoisier cognac. I poured it into the special tall glass for brandy and gave it to her. We started talking and I just fell in love with her immediately. She was unabashedly honest and forthcoming about her life. She didn't seem ashamed about anything.

Then customers started to come in. Eventually, a man sat next to her and asked to buy her a drink. I poured her another Courvoisier. Within a few minutes the man left and before he left, she told him tip the bartender. Then she looked at me and said take my brandy and put it under the bar. The next time a man buys me a drink give me that drink back and you keep the money. That was how our relationship started. She taught me a little con game.

She came back after 20 minutes or so looking just as perfect as when she had left. I found out later that her perfectly coiffed hair was a wig. She sat back down at the bar and asked me for some ice water. In no time another man came in and we went through the same scenario. I got the drink from under the bar kept the money for the drink. She reminded him to tip me. She was a force of nature, beautiful and intelligent.

That was my first up close introduction to the world of prostitution. Nikki was dating a very famous basketball player at that time. He was married to his first wife then, therefore the affair. He paid for her apartment in New York. He had a game in Scranton that weekend at the CYC. He toured with the Harlem Globetrotters. The team combined comedy as well as great athletic ability in their show. They were a world-famous exhibition basketball team. He's not alive so I can name him, Meadowlark Lemon. He and Nikki were scheduled to have a romantic rendezvous at the Casey.

She came in two days earlier to make some extra money. I asked her since he was rich, why didn't she just let him take care of her. She told me a woman should always have her own money.

I grew up watching Leave it to Beaver and The Donna Reed show. Housewives wore pearls and high heels while they vacuumed the carpet. I had been brainwashed by the propaganda that women needed men. They couldn't ever be entirely self-sufficient, especially if they wanted children.

Women's Liberation was still in its infancy, so I was mesmerized by this strong independent woman. That fact that she prostituted herself did not matter. If that was her choice, who was I to judge. She became my first female black friend.

The next night we went to dinner in the Hotel Casey

Gold Room. It was a very expensive place. I could have paid my way, but Nikki insisted on paying. She also tipped our bartender in the Gold Room very well.

Unbeknownst to me, she also gave him her room number in a note. So, she had a little fling with him later that night. After dinner, I went up to Nikki's room and we talked and smoked pot. She taught me a lot about life in the few days I knew her. She introduced me to the word "hinky". She was telling me a story and said "I knew something was hinky." When I questioned the word, she told me it meant something that is wrong or out of place. I don't think it was in the Oxford dictionary yet. After that, whenever I thought someone was dishonest or suspicious, I used that word. It made me feel very cool.

I really admired her independent spirit. I didn't care what she did for a living. She was just a unique person, one of a kind. I only spent a week in her company, but a strong bond was created. A bond that would resurface years later.

Meanwhile, Johnny and I decided to get an efficiency apartment on Spruce St. The only catch was the owner was very conservative. If she was going to rent to a couple, they had to be married. Johnny had a friend that lived in the building.

Her name was Franny. Franny was having an affair with one of the bar owners in town. I won't say his name because his family is still alive and I don't want to tarnish his reputation. He paid for her apartment. Franny gave a recommendation to the landlady and told her we were married.

We got the efficiency. Johnny was not just a bartender; he was also a musician. This is where I think I really started asking for trouble, dating musicians. Word of advice to the young, never date a musician. He played drums in a band. I can't remember the name of the band. But they were very popular around town. They played at The El Dorado.

This bar was owned by the DiLeo family and it was right across the street from the Hotel Casey. I was really in love with Johnny. At least I thought I was in love and of course I thought he loved me. It would be a long time before I understood that saying I love you does not necessarily mean I love you.

I spoiled him. I was making so much money at the Hotel Casey. I was shopping the best stores. I started to buy him clothes too. I thought everything was perfect with us. Until one day I came home from a shift at the Hotel Casey and the closet was empty of all his clothes. I can still remember my heart sinking to the floor. It was so painful to think that he had left me. We never had a spat or any disagreements.

I went to the El Dorado and sure enough, he was sitting at the bar with some floozy. I knew the girl from the bar scene. Let's just say I had one hell of an outburst. That was probably the first time I heard the line "it's not you it's me ".

My heart was shattered into a million pieces.

Nikki was in town so I went drinking with her to ease the agony of abandonment. Teary eyes and all. I put on my bright yellow mini dress, my shag wig and my go-go boots and tried to drink my pain away. You learn lessons in life by feeling the feelings. I guess I wasn't ready for the lesson yet. As they say, when the student is ready the teacher will appear.

# CHAPTER 14

# MEN OF MONTEDORO

It was widely known that Russell Buffalino became acting boss of the Pittston area after John Sciandra's death in 1949. The daily command of the Sicilian Men of Montedoro Mafia had passed to younger men.

Russell Bufalino had been born in Montedoro Italy. Shortly after, his father immigrated to the United States. settling in Pittston, Pennsylvania, working as a coal miner. With his mother and siblings, Buffalino entered the United States through the Port of New York in December 1903. A few months later, Bufalino's father died in a mine accident, and his family returned to Sicily. Buffalino emigrated to the United States again in January 1906.

He married Carolyn "Carrie" Sciandra who came from a Sicilian Mafia family. Buffalino worked alongside many Buffalo mobsters, some of whom would become top leaders in the Buffalo crime family and other future Cosa Nostra families along the East Coast of the United States.

These relationships proved very helpful to Buffalino in his criminal career. Family and clan ties were important to Sicilian-American criminals; they created a strong, secretive support system that outsiders or law enforcement could not infiltrate. A significant friendship was with his first boss, and fellow immigrant from Montedoro, John C. Montana.

Buffalino became the boss of the entire Northeast Pennsylvania crime family. A 1956 plane trip to Havana, Cuba, got Buffalino in trouble with immigration officials, as he improperly claimed U.S. citizenship upon his return.

Buffalino's family began to emerge from under the Genovese family shadow in the 1960s. The US attempt to deport Buffalino was derailed when the Italian government refused to accept him. Buffalino was one of the U.S. Mafia's most influential bosses until his death in 1994. He was engaged in labor racketeering, loan-sharking and gambling. The FBI believed he had a hand in narcotics trafficking. He is widely believed to have had a part in arranging the disappearance and murder of former Teamster President Jimmy Hoffa.

I became acquainted with a lot of rumored “mob soldiers”. I can’t authenticate connections to the Men of

Montedoro Mafia for all of them, but their actions and crimes certainly make me suspect that they were.

I cannot prove that Elmo (Al) Baldasarri was part of the Buffalino crime family. However, he was indicted on use of interstate telephone facilities with the intent to carry on an unlawful activity, and use of a telephone for the transmission in interstate commerce of information assisting in the placing of bets or wagers on sporting events or contests. I believe many of those calls were made on the public phone booth in the Hotel Casey Bar, while I was behind the bar.

Al Baldassari also had many legal businesses such as real-estate developments. Al developed Moosic Lake, Bellefonte Apartments and the land which ultimately became Mount Margaret Estates. He had a passion for music and dancing, which prompted him to open the infamous Orchid Club and Spruce Street Record Shop. He loved Bocce Ball, and had a Bocce court behind the Silhouette bar. This place was owned by his "Goomah" Helen.

The Hotel Casey was a known hangout for a few of these soldiers. They called the bar I worked at their office. There was a phone booth in the corner where they used to get calls. These guys would bring their mistresses (goomahs) on Friday night for drinks and dinner. Then on Saturday they would come in with their wives.

Cheating was a blatant and accepted practice. I started seeing someone in this group of quasi gangsters. Rocco was married and twenty years older than me. He couldn't be with me on weekdays and didn't want me to be alone when I closed the bar. So, he hired a bodyguard for me. My "bodyguard" Bob was the bouncer at the El Dorado across the street from the Casey.

Every night, he would show up to escort me across the street. I would have a few drinks. When I was ready to call it a night, he would escort me back to the Hotel elevator in the lobby. After a few dinners with Rocco, I received a call on that pay phone while I was working. An ominous male voice informed me if I kept seeing Rocco, I would be shot dead in the street. I stopped seeing Rocco.

I also briefly dated a well-known musician, Jimmy Tigue. Gosh, I knew a lot of Jimmies! The chemistry between us was explosive. He was a lounge player at the CiCi Lounge. He was also married but I think his wife must have turned a blind eye to his extramarital affairs. She was never at any of his gigs. Jimmy T. was a jazz musician, a cool cat. He taught me a lot about jazz music. I had not been interested in that genre before. Miles Davis and Billie Holiday, were his favorites. After we were both done working, we would listen to this music in his car and smoke a joint.

He was a good lover, but a little kinky. One night he asked me for a favor. He had a friend of his who was disabled. He wanted us to have sex in front of him. I guess voyeurism was his friend's thing. I said no! After that our relationship cooled down quickly. I didn't want to be with someone who wanted to pass me around like a plaything.

I was devastated by my breakup with Johnny. As a result, I did not want to fall for anybody again.

I made three pals and drinking buddies instead. Jimmy DeNinno, Jimmy Santoro, and Pete Petrillo.

Pete was related to one of the owners of the Hotel Casey. They were all wild and crazy, but so was I. I would get done bartending and meet one of them at Eagan's for a drink. Eagan's was right across from the Casey. It stayed open after 2 AM, illegally. You had to go to the back door and knock. They had to know you before they let you in.

You could order a steak at 2 in the morning. I can't count the times I came out of that bar with the sun coming up. Pete introduced me to exotic drinks, Chartreuse, Absinthe, and Mezcal (with the worm at the bottom of the bottle) just to name a few.

Jimmy DeNinno was 13 years my senior but he liked hanging out with the young crowd. He was a jeweler and always had several gold chains around his neck. He also had a perpetual tan, 12 months of the year.

Pete Petrillo was cute but kind of manic. I never saw him chilled out or calm. One night he knocked on my door in the hotel. He had a box with several cartons of cigarettes. He asked if I could hide them for a couple of days. I did. Pete did not have a steady job so I assumed he supported his life style by stealing or some other chicanery.

Jimmy Santoro was always very sweet to me, but he had a crazy side. A side that came out when he drank too much. He used to confide in me about his jealousy in his relationships. The girl he was currently dating at the time was named Doreen. She was a beautiful girl with flaming red hair and a gorgeous body. When she broke off the relationship, he did not take it well.

The next Friday night was a very busy night at the Casey bar. We had three bartenders on duty to handle the crowd, Butch Thuran, and a older waoman named Little Judy and myself.

Doreen was in a corner talking to a young man.

Out of the corner of my eye, I saw Jimmy S. enter by

the Lobby entrance. I looked at him and his face looked deranged. I knew he owned a gun. Instinct told me that he might have it on him.

I slipped out from behind the bar and grabbed him by the arm. I asked him if he had his gun on him. He told me yes and said "I'm going to kill that bitch!" I used all my powers of persuasion to talk him out of it and he left. I let out a sigh and went back behind the bar to finish my shift.

When I looked up there was Marshall (Peewee) in the lobby door entrance. He had seen the whole situation. He never spoke about it, but every time I saw him there was a look exchanged between us. A look that said we shared a secret.

These downtown boys were all a little crazy. Pete and Jimmy D. got very competitive over me. I would be in Jimmy's luxury apartment and Pete would call. I'd hear him ask if I was there. Jimmy and I were smoking a joint and listening to the album "Jesus Christ Superstar". I got on the phone and teased him about being jealous.

One night, Pete took me up to the roof of the Hotel Casey. We smoked a joint and then he took me to the edge of the roof. We were eleven stories up. He said, "Look at those people down there. They look like ants."

It wasn't what he said but how he said it that creeped me out. It was time for me to quit hanging with my drinking buddies.

# CHAPTER 15

# PROPINQUITY

Even though I stopped hanging with my three drinking buddies, I was still doing some risky things. One night, I was having drinks in Johnny Eagan's bar with a "new" male friend.  You could smoke in bars back then. I would pretend to smoke to look cool. I would buy a pack of Newports. Mostly hold the cigarette and pretend to inhale. The smoke would barely enter my mouth before I would exhale it.

We were both sitting in a booth holding cigarettes when he suggested a game. He held the cigarette to his hand for 30 seconds. Then told me to see how long I could last. Without hesitation, I held the ember to the base of my left hand. I don't know how long it was but he said I won. I still have the round scar to remind me of how reckless I could be.

I also did not realize that a pattern of self-harm was developing. Behavior that indicates a need for better coping skills. Several illnesses are associated with it, including depression, eating disorders, anxiety or post-traumatic distress disorder. Those at the most risk are people who have experienced trauma, neglect or abuse. For instance, if a person grew up in an unstable family.

Later that week , Curt, my deflowerer from prom, walked into the Casey bar. I was not working that night. He had filled out that once scrawny body and looked quite attractive. He bought me a drink and I apologized for being such a bitch when I broke his heart. He was charming and funny and I was getting drunk. We ended up at his place. His lovemaking had improved too.

However, when we were finished, he told me to get the hell out. He said, "I loved you with my whole heart and soul and you shattered that. I just wanted to even the score by rejecting you." I got dressed and left immediately. In retrospect, I don't blame him. I only hope that he obtained closure from our "one night stand".

I was 22 years old and getting tired of nightlife and being alone. My biological clock was ticking.

The Baby Boomer generation married young. Hell, I had already tried marriage before I was 21. I thought I could make a better choice this time. I had been dating musicians, drummers, and piano players. I had dated bartenders and bar owners.  I did not want to get involved with married men or “made” men. None of the men I was meeting were the “marrying type”. The pickings were slim in this town.

There is a theory called Propinquity. In social psychology, propinquity from Latin propinquities, "nearness" is one of the main factors leading to interpersonal attraction.

It refers to the physical or the psychological proximity between people. Two people working on the same floor of a building, for example, have a higher propinquity than those working on different floors. Just as two people who live in the same town possess a higher propinquity than those who live elsewhere. If I had gone to college or moved to Los Angeles, I would have had a vastly different selection of men. But the options were stymied by my parents, mainly my father. Scranton was my only resource for romantic relationships. I ended up marrying three times to men from Scranton. Not just Scranton but they all were from South Scranton.

The bouncer from the El Dorado who had been my bodyguard kept flirting with me. He was not my type. He hinted that he was a collection enforcer for one of the crime families. So far, my type always seemed to end in heartbreak. I told him if he had his hair styled and bought some nicer clothes, maybe I would go out with him. A few days later, he showed up looking like a different person. He cleaned up nice. We started dating.

Bobby Riccardo seemed like a safe bet. Everybody seemed to like him. For some reason, most people called him Harpo. I was never sure why. He said it was because of a boxer that was deadly in the ring. He thought it was Max Baer, who did have many nicknames. Bob had been a boxer in the Army or so he said. At any rate, I never called him Harpo.

Since, he was the bouncer and doorman at the El Dorado, I spent even more time there. Butch Thuran, Babe Tononi and Sonny DiLeo were the bartenders there. They too had a huge circular bar. Butch worked at all the bars downtown when needed, he was one of the best. There was also a dance floor with a disco ball. It was a lot wilder than the Hotel Casey bar. Drag Queens, gangsters, prostitutes, all types came in there.

I made friends with a transexual named Lovey. Lovey was always dressed to the nines from head to toe. Nails painted, earrings, sequin dress and high heels. One night we both needed to use the ladies' room. I was only in there two minutes when a girl came in asked if I was the bouncer's girlfriend. I said yes. She told me he had said, "She better get her ass out of there right now!" When I came out, he wanted to know why I would go to the ladies' room with a drag queen. I tried to explain to him that I thought of Lovey as female when she dressed like that. Gender never occurred to me. Obviously, Bob was very narrow minded. Soon, I would find out how toxic his sense of masculinity really was.

It was closing time and the staff was sitting at the bar having a drink. Bob challenged Butch to an arm-wrestling match. Even though Butch was on the skinny side, he was known to be quite good at arm wrestling. The first match he won. The second match Bob won. They had to have a tiebreaker. The two locked arms and both held on like they were fighting for their lives. After a few minutes, Bob put in an extra thrust. There was a sound I had never heard before. The sound of breaking bones. He had broken Butch's arm. I remember feeling sick to my stomach.

I didn't know anything about Toxic Masculinity when I was young. Even though, I had been victim to it many times. Men who had been violent, unemotional, sexually aggressive, and so forth. Men who thought that REAL men need to be strong and that showing emotion is a sign of weakness, unless it's anger, that is considered okay. The problem is these types hide that side of their personality when they are courting you.

Bob pulled out all the stops to woo me. Took me to the fanciest restaurants in Scranton, Dunmore, and the Poconos. He would order Chateaubriand and escargot to impress me. He told me he didn't really like that I worked at the Hotel Casey, especially the night shift. I had kept the efficiency apartment on Spruce Street that I had rented with Johnny. The room at the hotel was free, but I didn't want to lose the apartment so I was still paying rent there.

Bob wanted to spend the night with me. He lived over the El Dorado and I was not about to be that public with our relationship. If I took him to my room in the Hotel Casey, I would look like a prostitute. I told him that the landlord of the apartment thought I was married to Johnny and I couldn't risk losing the apartment. It so happened that outside the apartment window was a fire escape. Bob's solution was that he would come in through the fire escape so no one would see him.

A few days later, I had pulled a day shift at the Casey. In walked Al Baldassari. He always sat by the phone booth at the Lackawanna Entrance. This was a common thing. People would come and go, giving him money or slips of paper. The pay phone would ring and he would be making deals or I suspect taking sports bets.

That day he asked me if I would come work for him. He wanted me to work the day shift at the Silhouette. The thing about the Silhouette was that it was a cozy little bar that didn't do much business during the day. However, after dark it was known for being a gay bar. His girl Helen worked that shift. He said he would pay me more than I was making at the Casey. I really think Bob called in a favor to get me that job. Working the huge bar at the hotel was physically taxing so I said yes.

I really made decisions quickly in my twenties. In a nanosecond everything would change, although I didn't know it at the time. Every choice we make activates a unit of power. The struggle for power was about to begin once again.

# CHAPTER 16

# LIES AND LASAGNA

The First big lie. Bob took me to meet his mother, Connie. She had divorced Bob's father after having three children. She then remarried Robert Hoppel and had a daughter with him. I had graduated from High School with his half-sister. His mother had made a nice traditional dinner of homemade lasagna. She informed me that she rolled the pasta herself. I wasn't impressed. I used to watch my grandmother make pasta from scratch. She would hang the strips on the clothes line in the cellar to dry.

After dinner and a game of Gin Rummy, we went into the parlor. She looked at me incredulously and said, "What are you doing with him?". I said we were in love and getting married in November. That's when she told me that his name had been changed from Riccardo to Hoppel when she remarried. I was upset. First, because he hadn't told me himself. Secondly, because I wanted to continue to identify as Italian. Now I found out I would have a German surname.

The Second big lie. Bob told me he was taking me to Las Vegas for our honeymoon. The night before our wedding, he informed me the money he was counting on didn't come through. So instead, we were going to Washington, D.C.I had packed for sunny Vegas and now had to repack for frigid Washington.

After our short "honeymoon" I went back to bartending. I loved working at the Silhouette. Al had nothing but 40's music on the jukebox. Jimmy T. had already introduced me to some of the great jazz and blues musicians of that era.

My favorite on the jukebox was "I CAN'T GET STARTED" – sung by Bunny Berigan 1937, written by Ira Gershwin.

**"I've flown around the world in a plane**

**I've settled revolutions in Spain**

**The North Pole I have charted but can't get started with you."**

That song spoke to my soul. Stuck, not getting started was how I felt about my life.

The Silhouette lounge was so slow during the day, that my only customers were usually the Military Recruiters that had an office next door. We would play liar's poker with dollar bills and I usually won. I guess I had a good poker face. I would do the daily crossword puzzle from the Scranton Times every day. The Navy recruiter was impressed that it took me 30 minutes or less and that I did it in ink not pencil.

There was one guy that always flirted with me. His name was Terry and he worked at one of the banks downtown. He would come in after work and always had a funny story about one of the customers. Sometimes we would be the only two people in the bar. We had some deep conversations. It was nice to have someone to talk to that shared some of my ideas on life.

After a few weeks he begged me to have a drink with him outside of my workplace. I was planning on going out with my friend that night at a place called Papa Joe's.

He met me and my friend Sally at the bar. It was a large place with lots of tables and a dance floor. Sally had brought a date that night. So, there were four of us. Sally was the first to notice Bob barreling through the door. Terry got up and went to the men's room and I put his drink in front of Sally's friend. That was a close call. One of his spies must have told him I was there.

The lesson learned was never to sit with your back to the door. You always needed to see who or what was coming.

When he saw that I seemed to be the third wheel at the table, he calmed down. He gave me $20 and advised me that he didn't like this bar. He then left to go back to his job at the El Dorado.

That night I gave into my desires and slept with Terry. In the history of my sex life, Bob was a dismal failure, a one out of ten. I don't remember enough to rate Terry but I do remember he was tender and gentle.

After that it became very clear that Terry was more smitten than I. He would tell me that at home he couldn't stop thinking of me. He would pretend to read the newspaper, but he was really fantasizing about me. I had been hearing these tales from supposedly love-struck men since I was sixteen.

I let him know that it was a one-time thing and would never happen again. Disillusioned, he vowed he could not frequent this place any longer. If there was no hope for us, then there were only painful memories for him. He never came back. Ciao bello.

On Sundays when the bar was closed. Al and Helen would have us over to hang out at the bar. There was a Bocce court out back. Bocce, also known as Italian lawn bowling, is one of the most widely played games in the world and is one of the oldest yard games. Best known in Italy, where you may see a group of retired Sicilians gathered in a town square for a daily afternoon game.

We would play Bocce ball and Helen would make Polenta. Even though I grew up in an Italian house I had never tasted it. Polenta is a northern Italian dish made of corn meal. Freshly cooked, polenta is soft and creamy, like porridge or grits, and makes a terrific bed for tomato sauce. My family was from Southern Italy so I guess it was not as popular there.

Bob continued to make an erratic income as a "hustler". One of his scams had a buddy of his go into a bar and start playing pool. He was quite good and would win. At that time if you wanted to play the winner, you put a quarter on the table. Bob would come in and pretend not to know his buddy. He would put a quarter on the table for the next game. Then he would lose badly. The next game, the onlookers would want to bet on the game. Of course, they bet on the first guy who had won three games in a row. Bob would take their bets and then thrash his buddy. He would get all their money and leave and meet his cohort later to split the take.

Bob was a con artist and a gambler. But he wasn't very good at cards so he cheated. He learned how to mark cards and read them. He would spend hours making little bends, crimps and tiny pinprick bumps known as "blisters", resembling Braille script. He might also alter the designs on the backs of the cards. He used various scratches, to add or remove lines of patterns. He even had a deck that he sealed up as if it was a new deck, just in case the players were getting suspicious.

One night we were playing Gin Rummy, just the two of us. He won game after game. Now I am pretty good at Gin Rummy so I couldn't understand how I kept losing. When we went to bed that night, he confessed that he had been practicing his mark reading skills. I was furious.

His cronies would not play poker with him. They didn't trust him, but he would always find a sucker or two. We lived upstairs of my parents. He ran a weekly card party. One of the players, Sonny was a paraplegic. Bob would carry him up the stairs to the game, then take all his money by using marked cards.

He also ran poker games for some of the downtown crew. He would take what's called a vig. Vigorish (also known as the cut, the take, the margin, the house edge or simply the Vig). So, whether the players won or lost, he would win. His job was just dealing the cards, he wasn't allowed to play.

The El Dorado changed its named and remodeled when disco became popular around 1971. The new name was The Fantasia. A dance floor complete with a silver disco ball was installed. They had a coat check room. Corky, one of the owners said I could charge a dollar a coat and keep the charge and all my tips. It was a tiny room located between the entrance where Bob collected the entrance fee and the 'mezzanine'. The mezzanine to my left was a raised section of tables for people that didn't want to sit at the bar.

One night a girl was having a bachelorette party. She kept giving Bob glasses of champagne. Bob was not a big drinker, but when he had too much to drink, he would get mean. Also, he was 6'4 and 250 pounds, it was a little difficult to control that big a person. I asked her to stop giving my husband drinks because he was starting to get mean to me.

She called me a bitch and threw her champagne in my face, glass, and all. My eyes were stinging from the alcohol and my blouse was wet. I saw red. I was on the mezzanine in two seconds' flat. I grabbed her by the hair and ripped her top off. Sam and Babe jumped over the bar to pull me from her. Everyone stayed clear of me after that night.

We didn't have a lot of friends outside of the bar night-life. Bob and I went to a house party with a couple we met at the bar one night. After some drinking and pot, they brought out a big bowl. Each guy threw his keys in the bowl. The intention was that the wife or girlfriend would pull out a pair of keys. Whoever the keys belonged to would then go to another room or the car to have sex. Bob almost lost his mind. He grabbed my arm and we got the hell out of there.

The summer of 1972 I got pregnant. That had been the main reason I got married again. My biological clock had been ticking louder and louder. Bob had insisted I quit the Silhouette the minute I was pregnant. I still worked the coat check at the Fantasia on the weekends, but I had to promise there would be no more brawling with bar trash.

# CHAPTER 17

# CRIMES AND MISDEMEANORS

There a few famous people from Scranton besides President Joe Biden. One of them was Jason Miller, who starred in the 1973 horror film The Exorcist. His family moved to Scranton in 1941, where Miller was educated at St. Patrick's High School and the Jesuit-run University of Scranton, where he received a degree in English and philosophy.

New Year's Eve 1974, Bob was bartending at Preno's Restaurant and Bar. I had the freedom that night to go for a drink with friends. We stopped at Mooney's, a little hideaway downtown. There was Jason Miller, having a drink at the bar. I had run into him once before at another bar when I was single. I didn't think I made much of an impression. In case you are too young to know who Jason Miller was, his son is the actor Jason Patric.

I walked up to him and started with "So we meet again".

He pretended to remember our prior encounter and bought me a drink. I wanted to impress him with my knowledge of his career, that I knew more than just his role as the priest in "The Exorcist". I told him I really liked his performance in The Nickel Ride. I didn't know it at the time, but he had been offered the starring role in Taxi Driver but turned it down for The Nickle Ride. He said that might not have been the best career move.

In 1982, Miller returned to Scranton to become artistic director of the Scranton Public Theatre. His alcholism had gotten more progressive. His marriage to Jackie Gleason's daughter had ended in divorce. In 1972 he won a Pulitzer Prize for his play, *That Championship Season,* which also won the 1973 Tony Award for Best Play. In 1982, Miller directed the screen version of *That Championship Season.* Featured in the cast were Paul Sorvino, Martin Sheen, Stacy Keach, and Bruce Dern. His own film career was sporadic, as he preferred to work in regional theater. He died of a heart attack in a Scranton tavern, Farley's Bar downtown in 2001.

That night at Mooney's, I was loving the attention from this celebrity. He was flirting with me and buying me drinks. He said he hoped for a kiss at midnight. I looked at my watch and it was 11:30 PM. I had to get back to Preno's. So, I left and headed back. When I walked in, I said to Bob, "I left Jason Miller for you"! He was not amused.

The bartending gig at Preno's was supposed to be a permanent job. Bob had a great memory so learning the drink recipes was easy for him. But after a few months, the Preno's replaced him with one of the brothers. Family first.

Bob always exaggerated the truth to others. He was a liar and a con-man to the bone. He said things that were patently untrue to make people like him more. He would fold his money with the twenties on the outside and the ones, inside. You would see this wad of money, wow. Not knowing it was all ones except for the two twenties on the outside.

Bob would lie about everything. If we were renting a cottage at a lake, he would tell people we bought the cottage. I think he was always trying to look like he was more successful than he was.

The third big lie. A person of interest with ties to the Buffalino family backed Bob in buying an Adult Bookstore downtown. The catch was they wanted it in my name not Bob's. I think it might have been a money laundering operation. He was there all day and at night he would be out trying to con people. I was at home with our first born.

After a few months there was a robbery overnight at the

book store. The insurance company did not believe it was a genuine theft. There was an investigation and a warrant issued for my arrest for fraud. Bob and his partner said don't worry, nothing will happen. I was named as the defendant. My name was in the newspaper. As promised the case never went to trial, but my good name had been tarnished for life.

I became pregnant again with our second daughter. Even with all his hustling and hours spent away from home there wasn't much money. We had moved after Bob had an argument with my father. We were living on the first floor of an apartment building on Pittston Avenue. There was a pizza place next door. I was making artificial floral centerpieces and displaying them in the pizza parlor, to make some money.

I had gained a lot of weight after two pregnancies in 18 months. A doctor put me on diet pills. Two blue & oranges, two green and two yellow capsules. I could not tolerate that much speed. Bob told me people would pay good money for these pills.

I started selling them when I worked in the coat check room. The pills had nicknames. The blue and orange capsules were the strongest. They were called Hojo's because they were the same colors as the Howard Johnson restaurant chain. They were the most expensive at two dollars a pill. In today's currency that would be about $6. The other pills were a dollar each.

Two of the doctors that sold these drugs ended up in jail. However, not before years of doling out amphetamines to anyone who asked. It helped if you were overweight and didn't look like a drug addict. I made an income from those pills for several years.

I never felt like a criminal, even though I was literally a drug dealer. I was following the philosophy of Jeremy Bentham, "the good will have an incontestable utility over the evil." The most common example was if a beggar, pressed by hunger, steals from a rich man's house a loaf of bread, which perhaps saves him from starving. I needed to take care of my children using any means available.

**Life's not black-and-white. Sometimes the ends justifies the means.**

**Emily Giffin**

# CHAPTER 18

# HIERARCHY OF NEEDS

Inconsistency became a normal part of my life after I married Bob. When we moved into the place next to a pizza parlor, it was incongruously right next door to my parents. The apartment building had several floors with the pizza parlor next to our first-floor apartment. I had worked in the insurance field and knew the importance of renters insurance. I had taken out a $10,000 policy.

We were only there a few months when the pizza place had a big damaging fire. Luckily, I was not home. I was pregnant with our second child and was taking a nap with my toddler. My friend Carol showed up and we went for ice cream. I returned to find the building on fire and my mother crying in the alley. She wasn't sure if we were in there. My guardian angel at work again.

When the insurance adjuster showed up, I was pleased that I knew him. It was Frank Jenkins, who I had worked for a few years back. He told me, he would put it in as a total loss due to fire and smoke damage. Then he lowered his voice and said, “You can probably salvage most of it.”. I received a check for several thousand dollars. Now that we had some extra money, we were finally able to make that trip to Las Vegas.

My parents watched our daughter when we flew to Vegas. I was pregnant and it was unbearably hot in Vegas. Bob wasn’t very good or lucky gambling that trip. We were completely broke our last day there. We had gone off the beaten path of the strip to get a cheap dinner Downton. Walking to our hotel in the blazing heat, we saw a pay telephone. Bob put a quarter in to call a cab. The phone wouldn’t accept his coin. After a few tries, he became enraged. He began to hit the pay phone over and over. All of sudden, quarters started to pour out of it like a slot machine. We did have a good laugh about that crazy event.

We returned home and had to move again. We ended up a few blocks away in a four-apartment building on South Webster Avenue. Ironically, my friend Arlene lived in the apartment right next door. So, her little girl and my toddler played together and I had a friend to talk to. I had my second child. I did not want to get pregnant again so I started taking birth control pills. That meant I could not breast feed.

Unfortunately, the new baby did not do well on formula. She had colic and would keep me up all night. I would give her a warm bath, rock her and sing to her while rubbing her tummy. Finally, she would fall asleep. An hour or two later, her older sister would wake up. Their father would come in and go directly to bed. I was more than a little tired.

One day a man knocked on the door and told me he was here for the TV. I asked what he was talking about. He said Bob owed him money and told him he would give him the TV. I promptly informed him that was not going to happen and slammed the door in his face. Bob was not only not making money gambling, but was losing and obviously a lot.

I had not been able to wear my diamond wedding ring after I had my second child. My hands were still very swollen. I was trying to sell things to make ends meet. A couple came to look at the bassinet, which was now too small for my youngest. They bought it and I was able to pay the electric bill.

A few days later I noticed my ring was missing from the bedroom dresser. When I told Bob, he said that the couple must have stolen it. Instinctively, I knew that he must have taken it and hocked it. More lies.

I had to go on public assistance and get food stamps. To qualify I had to state that he did not live with me. That was not far from the truth. He was hardly ever home.

I was at the end of my rope with Bob. I demanded he go to marriage counseling with me. If he didn't, I would leave him. That was a futile threat at the time. He agreed and I made an appointment with Catholic Social Services. The young man, Paul, was very compassionate. He told us to each take a turn speaking about how we felt.

I went first and poured my heart out. When it was Bob's turn, he said nothing. Absolutely nothing. The counselor said maybe we should try individual sessions first. I think he was trying to get Bob to trust him. Bob went one time. I kept going.

After a few months the counselor, Paul, could see that I was in an untenable situation. He said even though this is a Catholic Agency, I need to give you some controversial advice. You need to leave him, go to college, and reach your potential. He then tried to explain Maslow's hierarchy of needs.

Abraham Maslow suggested that people are initially

motivated by a series of basic needs called the hierarchy of needs. Maslow states, "Self-actualizing people are gratified in all their needs , food, shelter, affection, respect, and self-esteem. A person has to first successfully navigate the hierarchy of essential needs . Once they have satisfied all their basic needs, Maslow proposed they then travel "a path called growth motivation".

I was still struggling with those basic needs. I had been pushing that boulder towards the pinnacle of the mountain for years. I would never attain self-awareness and self-actualization , at this rate. I was still concerned with money for food, my safety and begging for love and attention. How could I fulfill my potential while I was in survival mode?

If the hierarchy had to be attained in order, I was not going in the right direction for self-realization. He pointed out that I was trapped in a marriage that would keep me from fulfilling most of those higher needs.

I went home and pondered what he told me. I had never lost the desire to go to college. If I was staying in this marriage because of the children, that was not enough. Part of my low-self-esteem came from being overweight. I had gained over 50 pounds since I got married. The first thing I would do was lose the weight. I stopped eating junk food and went to bed hungry every night for a year. I lost the weight.

I was watching TV one night, alone as usual, and there was a knock on the door. It was Nikki, the friend I had met in the Hotel Casey. She looked sick and even thinner than before. She told me that she had been diagnosed with Tuberculosis. She wanted me to know that before I let her in. The bacteria that cause tuberculosis is spread from one person to another through tiny droplets released into the air via coughs and sneezes. Once rare in developed countries, tuberculosis, infections began increasing in 1985, partly because of the emergence of HIV, the virus that causes AIDS. The kids were asleep and I was so happy to see her. She sat as far away for me as possible.

We talked for hours. Some people you feel such a bond with. You may not see them for years, but the connection is still there. Neither Nikki or I had the life we had hoped for.

Meadow Lark Lemon was no longer in her life. After divorcing his first wife, he had become a born-again Christian. He married a woman with similar beliefs and fathered 10 children.

Those carefree days of drinking and disco seemed so distant. A lot can change in four years. I told her I was planning to divorce Bob and go to college. She was very supportive and absolutely validated my decision.

The last thing she said to me was "Dependency is weakness". I never saw Nikki again. I heard she died a few years later.

**"The flame that burns Twice as bright burns half as long."**

**— Lao Tzu**

# CHAPTER 19

# COLLEGE GIRL

I applied for college tuition from the State. As a single mother of two they would pay my full tuition. They would also give me money for transportation. I submitted an application to the University of Scranton which was now a co-ed school. They tested me and gave me 6 credits for life experience. I was accepted and enrolled as a business major. I then looked for an affordable place to live. I found a home that was a split level. The owners would rent out the bottom half to me.

Now the hard part, telling Bob. I told him I could no longer put up with his control and jealousy. Also, that he was never home and we couldn't pay the bills. He did not take it well, but he did not try to stop me from leaving.

I was able to get the girls in day care also government paid. Unfortunately, they had to go to two different places because of age requirements. I also had not received the money for the car yet. My day started with getting them up and dressed. Then we would walk down the hill to the first day care. Drop off my oldest daughter. My other daughter and I would wait for the city bus on the corner. We would ride the bus to the second day care a few miles away.

My youngest was not happy about it so the drop off took a little longer. She was three and a half and took quite a tantrum each morning. I felt just awful until one of the aides told me to look in the window after I left. Sure, enough she was playing happily with blocks. She just had a flair for the dramatic.

I then walked about a mile to the college. I would go to classes and try to get some of my homework and studying done. No internet then. Research meant the library, and microfiche tapes.  Microfiche is a piece of film cut to a specified size and shape usually approximating a library catalog card. Used to store catalogs, bibliographies, newspapers, and media just too voluminous to keep in a standard library.

About 330 PM, I would start the return home. Walk the mile to the one daycare. Wait on that corner for the bus. Get off at the other daycare and then the three of us would walk up the hill home. The girls would be fed dinner, given a bath and then to bed.

Now, I could study some more. At the time, I allowed

myself one guilty pleasure. I had a bong for smoking pot. Paralleling the bong phenomenon of the seventies and the rising "hippie movement," head shops and smoke shops gained momentum. Even in Scranton there was a place called 50 Kings downtown. That's where I got my bong/ water pipe. I would fill the bottom part with red wine instead of water and the pipe with pot. I would sit on the couch smoking and studying till my eyes started to close.

Believe it or not, I got straight A's. Although the college had gone co-ed, there weren't many females at the college yet. I remember one professor announcing," Only one student has received an A' in this class and it's a girl!" The anti-feminism was not hidden.

I really worked hard at studying and decided to go out with my girlfriends one night for a break. My parents took the kids overnight. When I got home, Bob was waiting for me in the dark. He pushed me around, manhandled and threatened me. I called the police when I finally got away from him. This was 1977 and domestic abuse was not being addressed.

Two women had been killed by their husbands in the past year in Scranton. They had both asked for protective orders. These orders won't necessarily stop an abuser from stalking or hurting a victim, they only permit the victim to call the police and have the abuser arrested if the order is violated.

One woman was stabbed to death the other was shot. I had a protection from abuse order on file. The police officer said he couldn't arrest Bob because he wasn't on the scene when the police arrived. The cop told me to buy a gun. He told me if this happened again to shoot him. But he cautioned that if I shot my abusive husband outside to drag him inside. That is no lie. I would buy a gun but not that time.

I filed and got a divorce. Bob still acted as if we were married. He had spies everywhere. If I did have a date, he would find out and show up. He would proceed to harass my date and threaten me. I didn't get too many second dates.

I was on campus one day and he tried to hit me with his car. He literally drove over the beautiful grounds of the quad to terrorize me. It was working. I was getting very stressed. I needed to get a gym credit. I was 28 and not very athletic. The University of Scranton had a gun course that they would count as a gym. Perfect. The instructor had been a green beret in the military. He taught me how to shoot a handgun and a rifle. Those classes not only taught me how to shoot, but took away any fear of guns.

That would turn out to be crucial knowledge.

# CHAPTER 20

# THREE MILE ISLAND

The money came through that allowed me to buy a car. I bought a baby blue 1972 Mercury Cougar. I loved that car. I was able to drive the girls to day care and myself to campus. It certainly relieved some of the burdens of being a single mother. It was still hard to keep food on the table. Every month it seemed the cupboards would be bare before the food stamps were due.

Then the universe sent me an angel in the form of a corner store owner. I started to buy a few things at a little corner store by my apartment. The owner saw that I was struggling. He would let me get a few things on credit every month. Then when my check came the first of the month, I would pay my tab.

I managed to finish two years at the University of Scranton. The constant harassment and threats from Bob were wearing me down. I remember one night I found myself on the floor, unable to breathe. I managed to call my father. He talked to me until I could calm down. That might have been my first experience with a panic attack.

I thought the solution would be to attend college out of state. But In order to keep my assistance, food stamps, child care etc., I had to stay in Pennsylvania. I applied to Wilson College for women in Chambersburg.

Wilson College is a private, Presbyterian-related, liberal arts college. Founded in 1869 by two Presbyterian ministers, it was named for its first major donor, Sarah Wilson of nearby St. Thomas Township, Pennsylvania, who gave $30,000 toward the purchase of the land.

For 144 years, Wilson operated as a women's college. Unfortunately, January 1979 they were in severe financial trouble. I did not know that when I enrolled. I was accepted and packed up just our clothes and a few toys. It was the middle of winter. I drove myself and two kids to Chambersburg, where I had booked a hotel room.

The next day, I was supposed to look at a trailer in Shippensburg. The hotel was a dive. We all slept in one bed. In the middle of the night, I woke up to find a cockroach on my youngest daughter's cheek. I brushed it off and then scoured the room looking for any more that I could kill off. I didn't sleep the rest of the night.

The next day we moved into our little country trailer.

It came furnished. I had enrolled the kids in the same daycare so no marathon drops offs. I threw myself into studying. I had no distractions. I had no friends, no family, no Bob. I stopped smoking pot and drinking wine. I needed my senses at full capacity.

I was studying one night after the girls went to sleep. This little field mouse came out of a corner and just sat in the middle of the room. I wasn't bothered by its presence at all. I was lonely so I guess I appreciated his company. I never saw a mouse after that night. If it had been a rat, I would have freaked out.

My parents had told me a story about their first apartment. It was down by the Lackawanna River. Joe wasn't born yet so I must have been about 9 months old. My mother came in to check on me and found a river rat in my crib. It hadn't bitten me. It was just sitting in the corner of my crib. My mother let out a scream and it scooted out of the crib and out the open window.

Although, I have no memory of the incident, the sight of a rat sends me into panic mode. Even if it's in a movie or TV show. I close my eyes and ask my husband to tell me when they are gone.

I was at Wilson a few months when the staff went on

strike. I would show up for class and there would be no professor. Written on the board would be “No Class Today, On Strike. “I could not believe my bad luck. Then one day, Bob showed up. He had tracked me down. If I could not get any farther away, I was doomed to have him in my life forever. I knew he had a friend in Harrisburg and he could just move in with him. Then he would resume tormenting me.

I needed a new plan. March 23 1979, I decided to visit my family in Scranton and mull over my options. March 28 The Three Mile Island accident happened. It was a partial meltdown of reactor number 2 of Three Mile Island Nuclear Generating Station (TMI-2) in Dauphin County, Pennsylvania, near Harrisburg, and 56 miles from where I was living. International Nuclear Event Scale rated the incident a five as an "accident with wider consequences.

That made one decision easier. I wasn’t returning to Shippensburg or Wilson College.

**"If you knew how a journey was going to end, you could afford to be patient along the path" Jack Kornfield**

# CHAPTER 21

# CATCH 22

I could not go back. I could not go forward. I felt stuck. Bob begged me to let him have another chance. We were divorced, but he was never going to leave me alone. I felt vulnerable and condemned to a life of bondage with this brute of a man.

He rented a mobile home in Honor Park ,Moosic PA. Nothing changed. If anything, he was even more controlling and jealous. There were no extras for my kids. I still had to struggle to get the essentials.

There was a Kmart nearby. I was buying our clothes from Goodwill, but always went to Kmart for underwear. I was not going to buy used underwear. If something was too expensive there, I would switch tags. I would look for a similar item that was on sale and then put that sticker on the item I wanted. This worked for a long time. Situational Ethics. Moral decision-making dependent on a set of circumstances.

The abuse was escalating. Bob would call me a whore and a slut. He would ask me how many men had I slept with while we were separated. There was a lot of pushing and shoving.

One Sunday we went to this big annual clambake. It was a political event thrown by the Democratic party. All kinds of people were there because the beer was free. I was sitting by myself while Bob circulated looking for the possible marks for his next poker game.

Eddie Evans came over to talk to me. He was someone I knew from working the bar circuit. I confided in him my plight. I told him I was worried that the manhandling was going to get worse. He told me "The bigger they are, the harder they fall". The best advice was to strike the first blow.

After that self-defense advice, I went for a walk. I was walking around the edges of the event. Out of nowhere came someone from my past. I was face to face with Jack Calvey, my ex-husband. Instantly I felt butterflies in my stomach. The chemistry was still off the charts, although I had not seen him in ten years. We walked into the woods away from prying eyes. I felt like it was a sign of some sort. After a stolen kiss or two, we made a date to meet at his house the next time Bob was at one of his all-night poker games.

The night arrived and I had made arrangements for a babysitter. I went to Jack's house. It was really his girlfriend Laura's house, but she worked nights. We had sex. When we finished, I started to cry. It was gentle and tender intimacy. I just thought about the good memories and blocked out the rest. Here was my savior. My white knight that would free me from this trap. I know it sounds crazy, but I was more than a little irrational at the time.

A couple of days later, I told Bob he had to leave. A very unpleasant battle ensued. He started packing, but every time he walked by me, he would kick me. I was holding my youngest child on my lap. She was crying and clinging to me so I was unable to remove her from the tantrum Bob was having.

After two or three times I said, "If you kick me one more time, I am not responsible for might happen". Of course, he kicked me again. Everything went black. There was a cordless phone next to me on the bed. With no forethought, I picked up the phone and shoved it right into his face. I broke his nose.

He stopped kicking me.

# CHAPTER 22

# BETRAYAL AND RETRIBUTION

I moved out of the trailer in Honor Park. The kids and I were now in a second-floor apartment on Capouse Avenue. Bob was still stalking me and harassing me. I was seeing Jack on a regular basis, one thing I knew for sure, Jack would protect me from Bob.

I was still selling diet pills to implement my income. I had an odd layout for the apartment. I had to go down a flight of stairs to answer the door. I had people call ahead and after we finished the deal, they were supposed to lock the door behind them.

This particular day, Jack was there. A guy came and when he left, he did not lock the door. He was bribed by Bob to leave it unlocked.

Like a tornado, Bob came up the steps and attacked me. Jack jumped up and tackled him. They were rolling around on the floor. Thank God the kids were at school. Jack seemed to be losing the fight. I picked up a coffee mug and hit Bob in the head with it. It wasn't enough to render him unconscious, but the fight stopped. He cursed me out, but left. My White Knight had saved me or so I thought at that moment.

When I had returned from my short stay in Chambersburg, my clientele for speed was very pleased. Even with the extra money from selling diet pills, it was still hard to make ends meet. Bob would not pay support.

The Department of Welfare even took him to court. I had to testify. His lawyer was Jack Brier. When Bob took the stand, the judge asked him why he didn't have a job. He said he had bad hemorrhoids. You can't make this stuff up. The court system was very corrupt and an old boy's school. The judge let him off.

I had a friend named Kathy that had a three-bedroom apartment in Green Ridge. She invited me to move in and split the rent. It seemed like an ideal solution at the time. My kids were just starting elementary school. I was hoping all the moving hadn't had a negative effect on them.

I was not seeing anyone else but Jack. His girlfriend Laura had kicked him out when she found out about us. He moved into a tiny apartment in South Side. I bought him dishes and sheets and a mattress from the Salvation Army. I wasn't ready to have him move in with me and my kids.

There was a woman who drank in the same bars as us. I wouldn't call Judy a friend, but an acquaintance. She had a barbecue one day that summer and invited us over to her house. There was a lot of drinking.

I went into the house to get some pasta that was keeping warm on the stove. I looked out the kitchen window to see her sitting on Jack's lap. I calmly walked out and dumped the bowl of spaghetti on his head. Of course, Jack said it was nothing, just harmless fun.

One day I showed up at his place unannounced and she was there. He was all flustered and sweaty. He denied anything was going on. When I would not buy that account of what I saw, he said he was going for a walk till I cooled off.

After he left, Judy told me that they were in love and they were absolutely involved. I told her she better leave and fast. I then proceeded to break every dish I had bought him. I cut up the sheets and ran a long slit down the mattress. I then put his clothes in trash bags and put them outside in the garbage can.

She was married to a roofing contractor that Jack had worked for. I went to her husband Gerard's house and told him about the affair. Judy and Jack were so scared of what her husband might do that, they hid out for three days. Then they both called their significant other to grovel, apologize, lie, and charm their way back into our lives.

The truth of the matter is that cheating and infidelity does not automatically cancel out love or what may be mistaken for love. I believed that I was safer with Jack in my life, even if in reality he was hurting me. He was keeping Bob at bay. I had a sense of dread that I would not be okay without him. I was also a sucker for his lies, "I'm so sorry. She meant nothing to me. " "I love you. Don't leave me. " You are the best thing that ever happened to me. You are beautiful". All those reasons and more caused me to forgive, forget and pretend that it wouldn't happen again.

Bob had been dating a waitress named Jane since I had moved to Chambersburg. He didn't stop when I came back. I later found out that even when he was living with me, he was still seeing her. He got her pregnant. He was now living with her. He decided to start taking the girls on weekends. He had a built-in babysitter so he could still go carousing till all hours. After a few weeks he pulled one of his dirtiest maneuvers. Instead of returning the kids on Sunday night, he kept them. He then informed me that he was calling welfare to stop my check and food stamps.

I would now be the parent that saw the girls on weekends. He underestimated how resilient I could be. I immediately got a job at Jim Theirs Dry Goods downtown. Basically, I was a sales person. One day Mr. Their let me arrange the store windows. I discovered I had a talent for retail window display. My windows seemed to bring more customers into the store. Spending weekends with the girls was great. I was able to get more quality time than I would during the week. Things were going smoothly.

Then my roommate decided to throw a party. She never asked me if it was okay. She was a bartender and she invited everyone from the bar and then some. The landlord was not happy. The eviction notice came in the mail a few days later. I called him and explained I had nothing to do with the party. I was a responsible person and would like to stay on. Surprisingly, he agreed to give me a chance.

Jack was getting some work as a roofer. I let him move in to help with the rent. Maybe that would keep him in line.

Easter Sunday, I went to my parent's house for dinner. Jack was persona non grata so it was just me. The doorbell rang as we sat down to eat. There were my two adorable little girls, suitcases in hand. The oldest spoke up. "Daddy said if you don't want us, we will go to the orphanage."

That's the kind of mean-spirited things he did. I am not a psychiatrist, but there was something majorly wrong with this guy. Was it a personality disorder? Sociopaths tend to lie, break laws, act impulsively, and lack regard for their own safety or the safety of others. Was he a psychopath? I read that a common sign of psychopathy is a socially irresponsible behavior, inability to distinguish between right and wrong, difficulty with showing remorse or empathy, the tendency to lie often, and manipulation. I only had Psych 101 in college, but his behavior did seem to fit the pattern.

I was thrilled to get the girls back. I had to quit my job at Jim Theirs to take care of them. They seemed very happy to be home and told me Judy had been very mean to them. I got them back to school in William Prescott Elementary in Green Ridge. I also signed them up for catechism at St. Paul's church so they could prepare for first holy communion.

One night Jack and I went out for drinks. The girls were staying overnight at my mothers. We liked this place in South Side called the Community Bar. We stayed after closing to have a nightcap with the bartender and one other patron.

It was after 2 AM when we left. We walked to our cars parked on the street. Suddenly a car came out of nowhere. The driver left the car running in the middle of the street. The door opened and it was Bob. Before anyone could stop him, he punched me square in my face. I hit the street unconscious for a few minutes. We called the police and an arrest warrant was issued.

I naively thought because I had three witnesses that this would be a done deal. At the Grand Jury hearing, it appeared as if I was the one on trial. The relevant facts seemed to be that I was living with my first husband and out drinking at two in the morning. Jack and our two witnesses also testified. It was thrown out for lack of evidence.

Furious, I went straight to the District Attorney's office. I said" I don't know what kind of bribe or deal was made, but I'm going to buy a gun for protection when I leave here". He said, "You should not tell me that." I immediately went and bought a 25-caliber pistol with a pearl handle.

**"People who confuse what they wish were true with what is really true create distorted pictures of reality that make it impossible for them to make the best choices." Ray Dalio**

# CHAPTER 23

# ONE FLEW OVER THE CUCKOO'S NEST

In October, Bob's girlfriend Jane gave birth to a baby boy. One of my friends called to tell me. I said one of the reasons I had stayed with Bob was because I thought he was faithful and had never cheated on me.

She decided to set the record straight. Bob didn't cheat on you in the beginning, but he did start when you became pregnant the second time. He saw Jane even before the end of our marriage. This madman was stalking me while having a "relationship" with this other woman.

Even though I had been divorced for over three years, I was devastated. I was angry with her for not telling me when it first started. I felt that if I knew, I would have left him a lot sooner.

Jack and I were partying with a lot of his roofer friends. One of those friends was Sean, Judy's brother. He was always trying to get me alone. The one time he made an actual pass and I just pushed him away. He was miffed that I kept rejecting him. I guess that was why he had to try and destroy my present relationship.

This night he told me that Jack and Judy were still seeing each other. I confronted Jack and he couldn't put on his liar's face quick enough. I slapped him and left with Sean. We drove around all night drinking. I usually didn't get sick when I drank but this night I did.

I had him pull the car over and went into some woods to throw up. I still was holding the beer bottle. Without hesitation, I broke the bottle on a rock and started tearing at my left wrist.

It was not a suicide attempt. It was a need for physical pain to alleviate the much deeper pain. It was also a cry for help.

The next morning, I had my sister Ann take me to Scranton Counseling Center downtown. I told them everything. The counselor asked "Do you think you might harm yourself or others?" I said yes.

I called my brother Joe and his wife Barb and asked if they could take my kids for a week. Of course, they said yes. They were moving to Arizona soon. They had three daughters. The cousins would have this last chance to be together.

I was admitted to the seventh floor of the CMC Hospital. This was the psychiatric ward.

At first, I looked around and thought I don't belong here. People were talking to themselves and doing crazy things like walking in circles. There was a young man named Tommy that I felt safe with. We played cards and watched TV.

After 24 hours Jack came to see me and we were placed in a visiting room with glass windows. Tommy kept pacing back and forth and giving Jack dirty looks.

We had ID tags on our wrists. Sometimes they would take us outside to the Nay Aug Park. I have small hands and wrists, so I could work the wrist band off. This way, if anyone I knew saw me, I could tell them I was a volunteer not a patient.

Before I was discharged, I got a call from Bob. He acted sympathetic and concerned. He didn't think Jack was good for me or the kids. I told him I would rather stay in this dark place with Jack then go back to a darker place with him. After a week I was released. My kids and I returned to our apartment on Marion Street.

One afternoon, Tommy showed up on my doorstep. He knew my name from the ID tags we wore in the hospital. It was easy to look me up in the phone book and find my address. He had developed a delusional attachment to me.

Jack sets him straight that it was a one-sided relationship. He told him that he should never come here again if he valued his life. That was the last time I saw Tommy.

# CHAPTER 24

# DENIAL

Jack's abusive behavior escalated. Now when he would come home drunk, he would wake me up. Then he would interrogate me and accuse me of cheating again. The middle of the night inquisitions was eerily reminiscent of my childhood. Sometimes he would push me around. Once or twice, he slapped me. One night I hid under the bed unitl he fell asleep.

Bob was still with his girlfriend Jane. Thankfully, the kids were with their father those weekends.

There was a couple that lived on the third floor, Vernon, and Colleen. Colleen looked as Irish as her name. Vernon was a big black guy who always had a toothpick in his mouth. The weekends that Bob had the kids, I started to go upstairs to sleep in their apartment. Jack would knock on the door and I would hear Vernon telling him to go home. No matter how surly or unrelenting Jack was, Vernon remained calm and never raised his voice. Jack would finally give up and go downstairs to our apartment and sleep it off. Vernon became my protector.

I had found a day-time bartending job in Throop. My shift didn't start until I dropped off the girls. There was after school day care at the school. Perfect hours. I also did well with tips. I had the perfect personality for a bartender. I could make conversation and tell jokes. I was also competitive and liked to win on the pinball machine. I was no pinball wizard, but I did pretty good.

I was drinking every day. I also was driving home after work and not totally sober. We were still living in the apartment on Marion Street. My brother Joe, who had moved to Arizona called me. The house in Jessup that he had sublet was empty. The tenant had left abruptly, leaving him in a bind. He told me if I took over the mortgage payments and gave him $5000, the house could be mine. I said OK, but I would not have the $5000 right away.

We moved to Jessup and started making a few improvements. There was an apartment upstairs and I rented that to one of my customers, Ethel. She was a sweet girl. Her boyfriend Fig came to My Place every day. He would order a beer and we would have a conversation about current events. He was an extremely intelligent man and a Vietnam veteran.

Fig was in a methadone program. He would light a cigarette and at some point, he would nod off. I would just let him 'nap'. When his cigarette was getting close to the end, I would place it in the ashtray before it burned his fingers.

Ethel and Fig were easy-going people. I don't know if it was trauma he witnessed in Vietnam or something else that brought him to the point in his life that resulted in heroin addiction. I do know that the methadone worked for him and he allowed him to be a responsible citizen. His girlfriend Ethel would watch my kids whenever I did a night shift at the bar. They loved her.

I was working at My Place about a month when I found out the owner of the bar wanted to sell. I envisioned an opportunity. He didn't own the building. He owned the liquor license and everything in the bar. He had what is called an immovable license. That meant the liquor license could not be moved to another location. He was asking $5000 for the business and liquor license. The landlord would also have to approve of the new tenant.

I had worked in a few bars to know about front money from machine vendors. Basically, they would give you the loan if you put their poker machines etc. in the bar. Every week they would take a payment from the take in the machines towards the loan. I knew several vendors that would front me the cash.

That night I told Jack. If we pulled this off, I would have the same hours. During the day I would take deliveries and keep the books. He could work nights. Of course, he was over the moon at the idea.

I contacted McGraw and Son Amusements and they agreed immediately. In came the poker machine, the pool table, and Space Wars video game. The quarters put into those machines would be used to pay off our loan. We passed the interview with the landlord. I lied and told him that Jack and I were a married couple. By Thanksgiving, we were the owners of My Place Cafe.

You would think owning a business and the prospect of owning a house would make my husband happy and content. But then again, his demons ran deep and dark. He was the oldest of seven children. Both his parents were alcoholics. Like my childhood, he was expected to take care of the six younger siblings as needed. There was physical and emotional abuse from both parents. When the Juvenile Court Judge offered the military as an escape, he took it. He joined the Navy and hoped to be assigned to a Patrol Boat, a small rigid-hulled boat used to stop and search river traffic in areas such as the Mekong Delta. Instead, they sent him to Naval Air Station Keflavik, a U.S. Navy station at Keflavík Iceland, located on the Reykjanes peninsula on the southwest portion of the island. Its main purpose was to secure North Atlantic air routes. Although his dream seemed more adventurousness than mine, it still was a dream not attained.

Many bartenders and bar owners are alcoholics. I am sure there are alcoholics that are good bartenders. Also that there are bartenders that are not drunks. That was usually the exception to the rule. I also knew recovering alcoholics who had very successful taverns. But many are directed to the bar business by the lure of "free" access to booze.

I was a functional alcoholic that could have successfully run our bar business. The one flaw in my plan was Jack. My husband was an atrocious bartender. Blinded by a fabricated sense of self confidence, he had a severe case of bigshotism. He would not take money for drinks from his friends. He would leave the bar to be with a woman or drink somewhere else and put just anyone in charge. He also had no common sense.

My shift was the moneymaking shift. I served cheeseburger and steak sandwiches for lunch. I soon made enough to buy Jack a used Volkswagen bus. Jack was not a good business man. He didn't like to charge his friends for their drinks. The one positive factor was that his friends liked to gamble.

The poker machine took in a lot of money. The pool table held lots of quarters every week. McGraw Jr. would come in every Monday. He was pleased with the income from the machines. Our loan was paid off in four months. Now I could start saving up for the down payment for the Jessup house.

We had a poker machine that was really the main source of income. The unwritten rule is if you don't know the person, as soon as they approach the machine, you tell them, "We don't pay out, it is strictly for amusement purposes only". Jack always failed to do that.

When a lucky stranger came to our bar and hit a Royal Flush on the machine, he demanded the $600 payout. Jack told him he had to speak to his wife the next day. Did I mention that Jack was also a spineless coward? He was unable to stand his ground unless drunk or holding a gun.

I called our vendors McGraw and son. Bill Jr. came down immediately to meet with me and check the machine to verify the payout amount. He gave me $600 in cash, but told me to try to talk him down to a lower amount. The way it worked the vendor and I would split the payout 50/50.

The lucky S.O.B. showed up as soon as I opened the bar. I told him; I really did not know him. He was not a regular at the bar so I really did not have to pay him. He responded that the bartender should have told him that before he had invested $100 into the machine. I offered him $300 and he grudgingly accepted.

When I gave Bill Jr. the $300 back, he informed me that my half of the $300 that was paid out would come out of my weekly take. I disagreed. If I had not got the compromise the vendor would be out $300. My mindset was that the $300 I talked him out of being my share. Therefore, I owed nothing. Keep in mind that I was on Food Stamps and in a shaky financial situation.

There followed threats and raising of voices. I knew this business very well. Vendors were hungry to get their poker machines in a bar. I just picked up the phone and called another vendor, J & R Amusements. I then called McGraw and Son and told them to remove their machines or they would be on the sidewalk in an hour.

An angry Bill Jr. showed up and removed their machines. J & R put in their machines and paid me a onetime sign-on payment. This all took place in a course of a day.

The following week I got served with a summons to go before the Magistrate for Throop PA. I was not one bit nervous. Like I said I was familiar with how the bar business worked above board and under. I was sworn in and asked if the vendor in question loaned me $600. I said no. I was asked if they had loaned me $300. I said no.

Then they called Bill Jr. to the stand. Now realize he could not give the real details of the situation. Poker machine payouts were illegal. He made up a story about why he loaned me the money.

The Magistrate then asked the all-important question. Did you get anything in writing?

His answer was no.

Did you get a receipt?

His answer was no.

Case dismissed.

This may seem unethical on my part. Let me refer again to the philosophy of Jeremy Bentham, that the end justifies the means. I was also still only on that first rung of the Maslow pyramid of self-actualization. I was trying to survive.

The life I was living was eroding my mind and soul.

**"Beautiful souls are shaped by ugly experiences."**
**Matshona Dhliwayo**

# CHAPTER 25

# FALSE HOPE

Jack continued the abusive behavior when he was drunk. More mental abuse than physical. However, I could see the escalation in the number of fights and the growing hostility when he was drunk. I told my oldest that if she ever saw him slap me to call the police.

Jack wanted to get re-married. He did not want to lose a good thing. Just my name was on the liquor license. So, it was in his interest that we marry. He said it was because we were soul mates. I should have known better. The Bible tells us a leopard can't change his spots. It's impossible for some people to change their character, even if they try very hard. So, we got married again that fall. I joked that Liz Taylor and Natalie Wood had also married the same man twice. Yeah, and Richard Burton was an alcoholic cheater and Robert Wagner was accused of killing his wife.

There had been a strange woman, from the Throop neighborhood that started frequenting our bar. She seemed to come in whenever she saw Jack's van. I never considered her to be a threat. She was very plain, unkempt and acted erratically. When we got married, she showed up at the party with homemade bean soup. Jack and I just looked at each other as I poured it down the sink. It was a very bizarre wedding gift. I joked that it may have been poisoned.

Two weeks later she called me at the bar. She said she was going to kill herself. One of the patrons knew her address. I immediately called 911. When they got there, they found she had hung herself. I was stunned. Was she that irrational that she had imagined there was something between her and Jack? Or was she another victim of his serial cheating? I will never know for sure, but I expect it was the latter.

True to form Jack could not change his innate nature. I believe Jack did love me until the day he died. His cheating had nothing to do with love. He would slip back into a very familiar pattern. I would suspect he was cheating.

Later, one of our bartenders told me terrible sexual things Jack did with women who were drunk and in the bar at closing time. Just like with Bob, I said "If I knew those things, I would have left him sooner." Up until now I had always assumed the sex, he had was consensual sex.

He was coming home from his shift drunker and more abusive. False hope and denial are such strong factors in a dysfunctional relationship. Cheaters know exactly what powerful manipulation tools hope and denial are. The goal of a cheater is usually to keep the wife and still have flings. "Have the cake and eat it too." Jack wanted it all, the cake (My Place) and the affairs and the marriage. Eternal optimist and damaged creature that I was, I still thought things could change.

Cheaters will use their fake remorse after each slip to keep you on the hook. They will feign regret, cry, say they can't live without you. They may even go to couples counseling. Jack used all the tools and then some. Because being alone is so frightening to most humans, we would rather stay in the muck then be on our own. Incredibly, I still held onto hope that things could change.

And when hope fails, there is always denial.

# CHAPTER 26

# DEATH BY A THOUSAND CUTS

Knowing the difference between physical attraction and love was still a grey area for me. Attraction can make you go crazy about someone only while the lure persists. Once it is over, you won't even miss that person. However, when you are in love with someone, you miss him/her even after years of break-up or separation. The fact that Jack and I had been drawn back together after ten years had convinced me we must be soul mates.

I had a very good friend that told me that Jack was an alcoholic. I remember how strong my denial was at the time. Much later in life, I came to realize that not only was he an alcoholic but a sex addict.

By way of a definition, "sex addiction" is described as a compulsive need to perform sexual acts in order to achieve the kind of "fix" like alcoholism or someone with opiate use disorder gets from using opiates.

There's also a common belief that "once a cheater, always a cheater"—that it's only a matter of time before it happens again. Assumptions like these ignore the complicated web of considerations that go into deciding what to do after infidelity is revealed.

Esther Perel, noted relationship therapist, wrote a book called "State of Affairs: Rethinking Infidelity." It encouraged people to try to understand how and why affairs happen, but also how a relationship might get better—with lots of work—after infidelity. In practice, it tends to be uncommon for a relationship to survive several instances of cheating.

Serial cheaters are exactly what their title describes: a person who cheats not only once, but multiple times within a relationship. Serial cheaters are usually personality disorders on the narcissistic borderline, sociopath spectrum. Their empathy synapses don't fire. They're wired wrong.

Dr. Susan Edelman ultimately defines serial cheating as "a continuous pattern of seeking out sexual relationships with people other than you partner, without your partner being OK with it." The key piece of the definition is the lack of agreed consent from partners, and this is what makes cheating different from open relationships or throuples. Deception is the key part of cheating.

Jack was a serial cheater. He was deeply, profoundly fucked up. Personality disorders do NOT get better. These people congenitally lack the ability to connect intimately with you. They fake it. They may look human, but they are really wolves in sheep's clothing. They're predators. I asked Jack to go to couples counseling. We made it as far as the reception desk before he hightailed it out of there.

Being cheated on has lasting effects. It can be challenging to engage with intimacy in a healthy way. Especially if a person has other challenges within themselves that they have yet to unpack.

I was starting to feel a sort of rage with each discovery of infidelity. I had an intense urge to seek revenge. I had screamed and cried. I had cut up his clothes and threw things at him! Those types of reactions weren't enough to quell the rage that was welling up inside me. Revenge is a primitive impulse and I was feeling pretty primitive.

When a person is scorned by his or her cheating spouse, more ancient parts of the brain like the amygdala and ventral striatum are the first to react. The amygdala notes the threat, while the ventral striatum notes how good it would feel to react. From there it's up to the prefrontal cortex, a more sophisticated region of the brain responsible for social behavior and self-control, to intervene. Based on my previous choices my prefrontal cortex seemed impaired. It was inevitable that I would carry out some type of revenge.

I had a new weapon in my arsenal for revenge. I saw how deep I had hurt Jack when I was the one cheating. Fidelity was no longer considered a valuable trait for this marriage. No, one upmanship was the way to go. You stay faithful and so will I. But if you cheat, be prepared for the consequences.

After, Jack saw how close I came to walking away with someone else, he was scared. He bought me a gold heart necklace and told me he would never hurt me again. I didn't believe him, but I still wanted us to be together.

Shortly after choosing him over Jackie B. a former paramour popped into My Place Café. It was late and I was getting ready to close. In came the Irish heartbreaker, Johnny Donahue. I closed the bar and the two of us drank Dewar's scotch while reminiscing about the seventies. We made love that night on the barroom floor. Afterwards, I told him that this was just a one-night nostalgic situation. I didn't want to see him again.

Johnny left and I drove home to Jessup. When I got

there, I realized my heart necklace was missing. I hoped I'd find it the next day when I opened the bar. I needed to find it before Jack. I went in early and there it was on the floor where Johnny and I made love. Crisis averted.

Saturdays I would get a babysitter and hang out at the bar. That was one night that I could be sure that the money would make it to the cash register. Near closing time, in walked Jack's ex. The girl he had left to be with me, Laura. She was taller and built bigger than me, but that didn't intimidate me at all. I made conversation with her and was polite since she was there as a customer.

She stayed till closing. The three of us left by the back door. Jack, then me and Laura behind me going down the four steps into the parking lot. Suddenly, she kicked me hard and I went flying. Now, we were having a physical altercation in my parking lot. She fought dirty too. At one point, she bit my breast. She was grabbing my hair and scratching like a feral cat.

I went into survival mode. Seeing nothing but red, I grabbed her hair on each side of her face. I banged her head three times on the pavement. I could have killed her with that move, but I didn't. She gave up and struggled to get to her car, leaving behind a trail of curses.

Lucky for her my pearl handed Smith & Wesson 38 stayed in my purse. I had won that fight. He might be a cheater but he was my cheater.

**"There is hardly any activity, any enterprise, which is started with such tremendous hopes and expectations, and yet, which fails so regularly, as love." Erich Fromm**

# CHAPTER 27

# QUEEN SISYPHUS

One night after working a night shift and having quite a bit of vodka, I had a small accident. I was driving by a popular bar on Church Street. A car parked on the street opened their car door without a thought of oncoming traffic. I swerved and barely dinged the driver's side door. I kept going. I did not stop. When I got home, Jack started an argument and slapped me. My nine-year-old called the police.

When they came and saw the powder blue cougar in my driveway, they asked if I had driven it in the last hour. Of course, I lied.

A few days later I was served with a warrant for leaving the scene of an accident. Luckily, I had some political acquaintances. One of them, Tony Shawn was a regular at my bar. I asked him for a favor in getting me out of this jam. He must have been owed a favor up the ladder. He got me Attorney Thomas Munley, pro bono, who was an important lawyer at the time.

Attorney Munley showed up on the day of my hearing in the Magistrate's office. He gave me a stern look and said, "You just sit there and let me do the talking". He proceeded to approach the bench. No one could hear what he said to the Jessup magistrate. A few minutes later, he came back to me and said "Go home."

I was greatly relieved not to have repercussions for that accident. However, not relieved enough to stop drinking.

I had not been able to save any money to buy the house. I had to come up with $5000. The bar had done nothing but further erode our marriage and my mental stability the last few years.

I had noted when I bought My Place Cafe that the license was an unmovable one. That meant that it had to stay in that location. What I owned was the inventory, the good-will and a piece of paper that allowed you to sell liquor and beer.

I found a buyer right away. Many a drunk dreams of owning a bar. There were a few hoops to jump through. The Liquor Control Board had to do a background check on the potential buyer. The man who owned the building had to approve him for a rental lease of the actual space.

Meantime, my brother decided to move back to Pennsylvania and needed the $5000 immediately to relocate. I was to receive the money from selling the bar in a few days.

I told my brother the deal was off and he should just move back in to his original home. I would leave in June when the kids were done with the school.

I knew it was time "to get out of Dodge", in this case Jessup.

I found a nice mobile home in Honor Park Moosic PA. Yes, the same mobile home park I had lived in with Bob. It had three bedrooms so the girls could each have their own bedroom. Also, The Riverside School district was excellent.

The sale of the bar and the purchase of the mobile home finally coordinated and we moved to the next arena.

I was able to get tuition from the State to attend a Vocational school and get certified as a Medical Assistant/Secretary. I had acquired a Associate's business degree in 1971. Combined with this vocational certification, I could obtain a very good job. The school was in Carbondale.

Bob still tended to do vengeful things and we found out he had put sugar in the gas tank of my Cougar. Sugar is a scourge to car engines because it doesn't dissolve in gasoline. Sugar poured into a gas tank will get sucked into the fuel lines and begin clogging up parts of your engine's fuel system.

That evil act resulted in having only one vehicle. Jack was supposedly looking for work. His opinion was that I should take the bus to school. He said he needed the car in case there was a job opportunity. I agreed and began taking the bus to school.

The bus stop was at the Kmart several blocks from our park. I would walk in all kinds of weather and get the bus. I always got the same bus driver. A brash obese comedian named Walter.

Walter always flirted with me. I told him repeatedly that I was married. He still would ask me for my phone number every time I got on the bus. One day he pulled into the Kmart parking lot and I was the only passenger on the bus. The doors were locked and he said he wasn't going to let me go until I gave him my number. Exasperated, I said you give me your number. He did and I got off the bus.

Jack would periodically get jobs doing roofing. In some town's men stand on a corner and hope to get picked for a day job. Well, in our town the gypsy contractors picked up workers in the neighborhood bar. So of course, this was a perfect excuse for Jack to go to local bars during the day.

He also started buying guns. First a 308-caliber rifle to hunt deer. Then a 30-06 caliber also for deer hunting. I gave him a gun cabinet for Christmas that year. I wanted to be sure they would be locked up. He charged those two rifles on our Sugarman's credit card. Sugarman's was kind of like Walmart. He also bought a revolver.

We would go target shooting, which I did enjoy. Jack also would make his own black powder bullets. Handloading is an involved process. Reloading manual needs your undivided attention. Nearly two-thirds of the cost of one round of ammunition is in that little brass case that gets left on the ground. Handloading means you can send more ammunition downrange for less money. I was glad he had these interests if it meant less drinking. He did seem content for a while.

One day I went with him. He had just purchased the 30-06 rifle. I had previously shot the 308. I mistakenly assumed that the 30-06 would have less of a kick. It turned out just the opposite was true.

Scientifically speaking, a 30-06 will have greater velocity than a .308, but a .308 still has less recoil and is therefore easier to shoot for most people. I aimed at the target and pulled the trigger and the scope hit me right between the eyes. I needed a few stitches. The scar at the top of my nose reminds me to never assume.

We got a Black Labrador Retriever puppy and named her Babe. The girls loved him. I was starting to feel that maybe things could be good. My children were thriving in Moosic. I was almost done with my medical training and looking forward to a new career. Jack wasn't making much money.

I started charging our groceries at Sugarman's. We were headed toward a financial cliff. I investigated filing bankruptcy. I found I could do that and keep my mobile home and car. The VW bus that Jack drove and possibly buy a small car for myself.

I filed for bankruptcy and had to testify in bankruptcy court. Jack refused to testify, but the rules said both claimants had to be present. So, he grudgingly showed up and sat in silence.

In Greek mythology Sisyphus was the king of Ephyra. He was punished for cheating death by being forced to roll an immense boulder up a hill only for it to roll down every time it neared the top, repeating this action for eternity. I was starting to feel just like Sisyphus. I was tired of being poor and doing everything alone. I had been working since I was a child and had little to show for my labors.

I finished my schooling and got hired at Scranton Blood and Plasma Center. I was at the front desk and would do the finger prick and then test for the blood type. I had to start somewhere to get the needed medical experience.

Downtown Scranton was not the ideal place to work. There were a lot of homeless people there. Every week the homeless alcoholic men would come in to donate. They were not bad people, just unlucky and homeless. I saw the good in many of them. Two of those homeless men, Roger, and Stan, were always telling jokes and chatting as if everything was just peachy in their life.

Winter was coming so I brought some of Jack's old plaid shirts in for them. We talked about everything while they waited to sell their plasma. One of the topics was The Scranton Iron Furnaces. It is a historic site that preserves the heritage of iron making in Pennsylvania. Four stone blast furnaces which were built in 1848.

This is where these homeless men lived. Hard to believe, but I was about to step into another bizarre and senseless dimension.

# CHAPTER 28

# RUSSIAN ROULETTE

There was something about Roger that was intriguing. A Vietnam vet who had seen some horrific things as a U.S. Marine. The veterans of that war faced much criticism after returning to the U.S. The American public's opinion was divided. Some criticized them for losing the war, while others criticized them for killing innocent civilians. In any case, they had to live with the consequences. Combine that with a dose of P. T.S.D. and you have a walking disaster.

Many of these men turned to drugs and alcohol and lost everything, many becoming homeless. Stan and Roger were both vets. They were quite congenial and amusing personalities. I felt a great deal of compassion and connection with Roger. One day, he told me that we're going to get some beer and hang out at the Iron Furnaces. He asked if I would stop by and say hello on my way home from work. I did and it was just Roger, Stan, and me. I had a beer and went home.

I tended to be too open and friendly with people. I was

never judgmental of anyone's circumstances. They all had a story and a path that would lead them to where they needed to be at the end of that journey. So, a couple of times I stopped on the way home and had a beer with the homeless guys.

The YMCA and the Salvation Army allowed the homeless to take showers and get a meal. The two I had befriended always looked neat and clean. The only smell emanating from their bodies was alcohol.

There came a day when it was just Roger and me at The Iron Furnaces. It started to rain so I let him sit in my car. He made a move to kiss me and I let him.

After that kiss, I knew I could never go back to the Furnaces. However, it was too late to stop Roger from developing a romantic fixation on me.

I was at work at the Plasma Center when FTD came in with a bouquet of roses for me. There was no card so I assumed they were from my husband. When I walked in with the flowers, Jack looked very angry. He demanded to know who they were from. I told him I thought they were from him because there was no card. He firmly reminded me that anytime he gave me flowers, it was in person. I told him I must have a secret admirer. Jack threw the flowers in the garbage straightaway.

Of course, I now realized it was Roger. He started waiting for me after work. I didn't find him threatening, but I didn't want to lose my job. I told him I was afraid he would get me fired. Then he started waiting for me in the parking lot down the street. I firmly reminded him that I was married and didn't want to continue a clandestine affair. His reply was that if my husband met with him man to man, he would leave me alone.

What was it with this man-to-man nonsense? As hard as it was to fathom, I knew he needed that showdown for closure. Telling Jack was not as hard as I thought it would be. After all, his cheating score card was more filled in than mine. He was upset and angry. But he knew how determined Jack B had been at the showdown at My Place. He had been very close to losing me then. He reluctantly agreed to the meeting.

There was a bar downtown called The Dutchman. It was always quiet there. The agreed time was after I got off work, the three of us would meet. I walked in and Roger was already there. I went straight to the bar and ordered a double vodka on the rocks. Jack came in and I made the introductions.

Neither one raised their voices or threw a punch. Roger told Jack that I was an admirable and beautiful woman and should be valued as such. He wanted a promise that Jack would always be good to me. Jack told him in an annoyed manner that he knew how to take care of his wife. They even shook hands.

We left the bar to walk to my car in the parking garage. Jack realized that Roger was following us. He turned around and said "Look buddy I have been very civilized so far, but if you need to get physical, I will be glad to oblige." Roger turned and walked away. Although an ambiguous one, I now had another infidelity check on my scorecard.

I hadn't given Jack all the details, just enough to paint the picture I wanted. I had made it seem like all the advances had been by Roger. I certainly did not tell him about the kiss.

Just an aside: Years later, I ran into Stan downtown. I almost didn't recognize him. He looked healthy, clean, and sober. He told me a woman named Betty took him in. She literally picked him out of the gutter. She brought him into her home and took care of him and grew to love him. They were now married and he was a re-born Christian. Miracles do happen.

My realtionship with Jack was a sick addiction. Waiting for a miracle in my life did not seem to be the road for me to stay on. Infidelity is a betrayal, one that is deeply traumatic. It's normal to experience a range of complicated thoughts and feelings in the aftermath.

But what about serial infidelity? The pattern that Jack and I now appeared to have. There is a phenomenon called Hysterical Bonding. Juxtaposed with your agony and distress, lies the desire to reconnect, to be comforted, to win them back from their affair partner. The need to feel wanted can prompt a desire to reconnect sexually. This rekindled intimacy may feel new, different, or unlike sex you had in the past. That was us for a short while after every extramarital dalliance.

Our other problems were still there, lack of money, drinking, abuse, and mistrust. Jack's drinking was just out of control. I liked to drink at home, but he would start right after work and not come home till late at night. One night, he came home drunk and demanded dinner. I had made stew in the crockpot. When he began to eat, he made a remark that it was cold. I threw the crockpot at him. My long-repressed anger was about to erupt. We couldn't go on like this.

A week later he came home drunk as usual but surlier than customary. He took his revolver out of the gun case. He started to berate me about my failings and past indiscretions. He told me I made him feel less of a man and that was what led to his cheating. Then he held the gun to my head. I didn't even flinch. I had learned from my college gun classes that if the safety was on, the gun wouldn't fire. That was not the response he expected.

He then put the gun in my hand and held it to his head. This time he took off the safety. He told me to pull the trigger and I did. The gun had no bullets. He grabbed the gun and pushed me further back into the chair. He screamed "What if there were bullets in that gun?". I answered, "Then you would be dead". Now if there was a shred of sanity left in either of us that should have been the end of the marriage. But it wasn't.

You can't stay in an abusive relationship and not be affected by it. As a normal, feeling human being, it is not possible to be in such a situation and not be affected profoundly by it.

Jack was so much better at destroying my boundaries and pushing me beyond my limits than I was at keeping him in place. As always, there comes the straw that breaks the camel's back. Believe it or not I still needed one more betrayal to be the final catalyst.

# CHAPTER 29

# THE LAST STRAW

A wonderful opportunity materialized for me in the form of a new job. I interviewed and was hired by Dr. Sheldon a prominent dermatologist in Scranton. I was to be a front desk receptionist and medical secretary for his new partner Dr. Zenker. My income was greatly increased. Still not enough to be a one income family, but perhaps able to avoid bankruptcy again.

I was cross-trained to assist the doctor in small surgeries once a week. That was very exciting. Just to hand him the scalpel and dress the wound, made me feel very professional.

Jack had got a job working in a plant that made miniature golf courses. It paid pretty well, so I prayed that he would not lose this job. We would leave about the same time every morning after the kids left for school. We also got home at the same time. Surprisingly, he didn't get drunk as often.

Jack had a come from a big family. However, his mother had died and he didn't speak to his father. The matriarch of the family was Aunt Gloria Miller. She was a funny, unique woman who liked to drink Stegmaier beer. We would visit her and Jack's cousins Larry and twins Jimmy and Paul. The beer was awful but we would have a lot of laughs. Paul was dating a girl named Jeanne Atkinson at the time. Of course, we were all South Siders. Propinquity!

Sometimes Paul and Jeanne would hang out in our yard and drink. I was more friends with Paul than her. He was good-natured and quite amusing. Spring 1986 I was actually holding some hope for our family. Until the day Paul came over unexpectedly for coffee. Jack was out in the woods target shooting (or so I thought), so I was alone. He said he needed to tell me something.

Jack and Jeanne were having an affair. I was surprised since Jack was home so much more than in the past. Then he dropped the bombshell. Jack had been fired two weeks ago. When he left each morning, pretending to go to work, he was going to Jeanne's apartment. He usually got paid on the 15$^{th}$ and 30$^{th}$ of the month. How was he going to explain the lack of a paycheck?

I have felt rage in the form of color many times in my

life. Seeing black, when Bill Cerra tried to rape me, seeing red before I broke Bob's nose. At this moment I felt a white-hot rage come over me. I grabbed my car keys and headed to Jeanne's apartment.

The blue VW bus was parked at the curb. Just as I pulled up, Jack was leaving and standing in the doorway kissing her goodbye. I ran up the stairs, pulled back my arm and slapped him with all the force in my small body. The deafening sound the slap made caused Jeanne to gasp. I turned to her and said "Shut up or you're next." She looked absolutely terrified.

I ranted for a few minutes about what an ungrateful, scurrilous piece of shit he was. As I walked down the steps, I looked back at Jeanne and said, "You are not the first and you won't be the last." I then walked down to the corner bar to use the pay phone.

I called Paul first and told him that I had caught them. I said if he didn't hear from me in an hour to come to her apartment. I felt murderous and it scared me. Paul said he would be right there and not to do anything crazy. Then I called the police to tell them my soon to be "ex" was stopping me from taking my vehicle. I even called Walter, the bus driver, to have him calm me down.

When I went back outside, I confronted Jack and told him to say goodbye to his bus. The guys in the bar had realized something was going on and had come out to observe the unfolding drama. Jack moved towards one of the tires. I assumed it was to do damage so the vehicle would be undrivable. The guys walked closer and said "Hey buddy, don't do something stupid."

The police showed up and I informed them I was the owner of the bus. Jack told them it was his. The policeman asked him who was on the title. We had him there. Paul arrived and was relieved to see that everyone was alive. He drove the VW home for me.

The almost routine existence of cheating, lying and abuse had finally reached a limit that caused an earth-shattering reaction in my soul.

Despite the terrible behavior the last six years, I had still felt that we were soul mates and someday would get our act together. This last straw blew the lid off all the old, unhealed wounds that I thought I had successfully locked away. I saw my inner child standing naked and bleeding, feeling raw and vulnerable. The camel's back may have been broken but its soul was primed for rebuilding, ready for whatever it took for deep healing.

# CHAPTER 30

# DIVORCE PTSD

I never thought of my mother as that of a mirror, reflecting who I would become as an adult. Now I understood that she was my mirror. What her reflection showed me, that a woman should take all kinds of abuse and not leave. That a woman could have a husband that fooled around with other women and she would look the other way. {In my father's case probably men}.

She demonstrated coldness, aloofness, and lack of interest in anything that I loved. This was the basis for many of my choices. Low self-esteem, unworthiness, abnormal loyalty, fears. I did have a maternal mirror after all, but it was cracked and distorted.

The distorted example of relationships I grew up with caused me too stay much too long in both of my marriages. Enough was enough.

The next day I packed up all of Jack's belongings including his guns. I dropped them off at Jeanne's apartment. I was able to sell the gun cabinet which helped with that month's bills. Bills that had included beer, cigarettes, and gun accessories now would also free up some money. I called the car lot where I had purchased the VW and convinced them to take the bus back in exchange for what was left on the balance of the loan. Jack started calling with the usual crying, cajoling, justification etc. I think he heard something different in my voice this time.

I had my children, my home, my car, my job. I was alone, but in the best place in my life, a turning point. Jack's ex, Sharon and I agreed to still let the kids spend alternate weekends at each other's homes. I had grown very close to my stepchildren over the last seven years. She was a single Mom too, and it was nice to still have babysitting options in place.

As soon as I was able to take a vacation day from work, I took the girls on a bus trip to Philadelphia. The first vacation in years. They were not at all sorry to see Jack leave. Especially since during one of his drunken tirades he had kicked our dog Babe. A couple of days later the dog died. That was more than enough reason for them to have hard feelings for him.

Single again, but not looking for a relationship. My friend Sue and I started going to Pocono Downs every Friday. Pocono Downs had Harness racing. It is a form of horse racing in which the horses race at a specific gait (a trot or a pace. They usually pull a two-wheeled cart called a sulky occupied by a driver. Her family had some connection to horse training so we got to go to the stables and see the horses.

There were two jockeys, we got friendly with Bobby Williams and Ari Reynolds. We would have a drink after the races and soon we were invited to the weekly Jockey party. They would discuss who the three best horses were that week. Then they would speculate who should win, place and show. They let the girlfriends place the bets. My jockey never gave me money to bet for him. He was not that stupid. He wasn't going to take the chance of getting caught and losing his career as a jockey. He would just give me the heads up before the race so that I could bet if I wanted to.

I didn't bet a lot but I was glad to have the extra money when I won. Bobby told me before each race that he was in to come down to the paddock. If he gave me the signal then I should bet his horse to win first place. Now there was always the factor of the unknown. I would always bet to win, place or show. Each time I happened to go to the same cashier to place my bet. After a few weeks, this casher said "I realized who your boyfriend is. You don't need money at my window. Just give me your bet and I will give you the ticket." That was a nice scam for a few months.

Jockeys move on from racetrack to racetrack. Eventually Williams was on his way to another racetrack. It had been an exciting relationship but one with no future. My friend Sue continued her relationship and married Reynolds. I know they had a child but then I lost track of her. Years later I heard they had gotten divorced.

I was enjoying my job at the dermatologist's office. Dr. Sheldon took on a partner, Dr. Zenker. I became her secretary/assistant. It was summer and I usually sent my girls to St. Andrews Day Camp. This year they begged me to let them stay home. They were 12 and 13. They wore me down and I reluctantly agreed. What a mistake. They would be bickering at each other and call me at work to settle the dispute, I told them do not call unless it is an emergency. I also told them no one was allowed inside our home while I was at work.

A neighbor called me and said I thought you should know what's going on. Some boys have taken the screen down and are climbing in the window. I called and told my girls that the police were on their way. I said that I had reported that there was a break-in. Of course, I had not called the police but they believed me and so did the boys. Everyone cleared out. It was very stressful being a single working Mom.

To de-stress, I got in the habit of stopping for a drink after work. A place called the Nativity Club. A friend from the El Dorado days, James Minelli, was the manager. All I needed was to show up and he would buy my drinks. The bartender was a loud Irishman, Jerry Brier. My first impression was that he was brash and obnoxious.

An old schoolmate of mine came in and was surprised to see me. He said, "hey remember me, we went to junior high together?" This Brier guy yelled, "Hey, I went to school with you too!" I dismissed his declaration with a contemptuous glare.

Minelli liked being seen with arm candy. He was at least 30 years older than me and completely harmless. I let him take me to dinner a few times and buy the drinks at the club. There was never anything sexual. If I had had sex with him, it probably would have killed him.

I was in a place where I wanted to use men not have an intimate relationship with anyone. Both Jack Calvey and

Johnny Donahue had broken my heart. I had built a wall of ice around the core of it. No one would ever be allowed to delve into my heart and soul again.

Another place that was on the bar hopping list was Tony and Mary's. This was a real dive but the drinks were cheap. My sister and I would go there knowing we would be the best-looking chicks in the place. Our competition was burnt out drunks. When we had no money, I would call her and say "Let's go slumming".

I had got friendly with two guys there, George Parker and Pete Nichols. They were smart and funny. Just some people to hang out with.

Post-divorce drinking seemed like a harmless distraction, but it can, lead you down a road you're not prepared to ride. "A history of past trauma is a risk factor for developing PTSD post-divorce. In people with PTSD from past trauma," says psychiatrist Dr. Susan Edelman, "the breakup of a relationship can led to worsening symptoms of post-traumatic stress and psychological well-being."

I had a lot of traumas in my life. But I also had the will to keep living life no matter what it would generate.

**"Life is inherently risky. There is only one big risk you should avoid at all costs, and that is the risk of doing nothing." Denis Waitley**

# CHAPTER 31

# A SLOW HAND

The summer of 1986, I was just enjoying being single. The divorce from Jack went smoothly. However, Jack showed up at the courthouse which surprised me. He asked my lawyer if he was sleeping with me. That was a ridiculous question. Then he said to the divorce lawyer: "What if I told you, I had a gun on me?" The lawyer replied, "I'd say that's pretty stupid. If you pulled out a gun, one of the many laws enforcement officers present would shoot you." This was before they had metal detectors at the courthouse. He admitted that he didn't have a gun.

The only thing to contest in the divorce settlement was the mobile home. He signed it over right there in the hallway of the Lackawanna County Courthouse.

I wanted to celebrate that night but none of my girlfriends were available. I decide to go out alone. I picked Chicks Country Western bar for several reasons. It was in South Side, familiar territory. I would probably know everyone there. Also, it wasn't Jack's type of bar so I wouldn't run into him.

The doorman was a friend of my sister's named Porky. He was several years younger than me. He told me I didn't have to pay the cover charge. He got me a drink and a chair next to him at the door. The last thing I needed was another over-sized bouncer in my life. I decided to sit with him till I finished my drink.

A guy walked in that I had never seen before. There was a good reason for that. He had just got out of jail. His name was Ronnie Vaughn and he was very attractive. He also had that certain vibe, "je ne sais quoi" as they say in France. He had an elusive aura that made him stand out in a crowd. The look that he gave me said he was interested too.

This bar had a dance floor and a band. The band started playing Deep River Woman by Lionel Richie. Porky asked Ronnie if he would watch the door so he could dance with me. Before anyone could blink, I grabbed Ronnie's hand and said, "I want to dance with you."

When he put his arms around me and we started to dance, the chemistry was obvious to both of us. When the dance ended, he took my hand and led me down a back hallway. Once hidden from prying eyes, he kissed me.

His kiss was tender and slow. A kiss that conveyed deep desire yet had a reverence about it. A kiss that said, I know you're not a one-night stand. There was a seldom used side door. We slipped out that way so Porky would not see us.

A half a block away was Tony and Mary's. One of the bartenders lived upstairs and was having a party. We decided to go there. Gary would surely have some pot among other party favors. We got there and a joint was passed around. Later, after Chicks closed in walked Porky. He was not pleased to see us there.

We did not have sex that night. One of my rules through the years was never to have sex on the first date. I was counting this as a date.

Ronnie and I became a couple fast. He would be waiting for me across the street, outside the building where I worked. The first time, all my female coworkers checked him out through our seventh-floor window. They thought he was very handsome.

When we finally did have sex, I found out just how transcendent physical contact could be. He was slow and methodical. In my mind I would hear that song by the Pointer Sisters, "Slow Hand".

**I want a man with a slow hand**

**I want a lover with an easy touch**

**I want somebody who will spend some time**

**Not come and go in a heated rush**

**I want somebody who will understand**

**When it comes to love, I want a slow hand**

That was Ronnie Vaughn.

He worked nights so we could only see each other two nights a week. I would sometimes meet him for his lunch break and bring him food. He told me about his misspent youth and going to jail for the crime of burglary. He went on that the time he spent in prison was soul changing. He vowed to walk the straight and narrow from then on.

October was my birthday. He told me to make sure to meet him for his lunch break in the parking lot where he worked. I did and he greeted me with a very sweet kiss. He handed me a little blue box. Inside were the most beautiful opal earrings. I was impressed that he would buy me such expensive jewelry and that he did the research to find out my birthstone.

November, I invited him to my family home for Thanksgiving. I thought we were at a point in our relationship where he could handle meeting my crazy family. He said he would come but then at the last minute he came up with a lame excuse.

I then had him over to meet my girls. He was very awkward around him. I knew that he once had a serious relationship prior to ours. I also knew that him not wanting kids is what led to its demise.

The following week I called him from work to see when we were getting together. He broke up with me over the phone. He used the same line as Johnny Donahue, "It's not you, it's me." I was devastated to the point that I had to leave work.

The James Bond personality, confident, mysterious, and quiet was what had attracted me to him in the first place. However, I now realized that also included a fear of commitment.

Ronnie had begun to melt the wall of ice I had protecting my heart. But it was a just a romantic fairy tale. I berated myself for letting feelings of love seep in again.

I should have known that this heartbreak was inevitable. I was 38 and had three major heartbreaks. No matter if you are sixteen or sixty, heartbreak is equally excruciating and leaves you raw and feeling violated. The lesson learned was that I needed more than a wall of ice to guard my heart.

# CHAPTER 32

# BARTENDER'S ADVICE

I was confounded and confused about the breakup with Ronnie. In retrospect, I realize meeting my kids had been the decisive moment for him. He realized it was a package deal and he did not want something that complicated.

I turned to my old friend alcohol to ease the pain. During the week, I would drink at home since I had to work the next day. But on weekends I was drowning my sorrows in the worst dives in the city. I was not looking for male company, just cheap booze.

One Friday night, I was drinking with my buddies Pete and George in Tony and Mary's. Pete had a very jealous girlfriend named Linda who did not know me. When she came in and saw him sitting next to a strange woman, she became enraged. She picked up a bottle of beer and hurled it. I am not sure if it was meant for me or Pete, but it hit me. It hit the right side of my forehead. Hard enough that I almost lost consciousness.

Someone, ran down to Chick's bar to get Ronnie. It was pretty much known that he still cared for me. He came in and I called the cops. I filled out a report. I knew her name and I had witnesses, so she was in trouble. I should have gone to an emergency room but instead I went to Ronnie's apartment. The kids were with my parents so I stayed the night.

The next day I got a call from this Linda. She apologized and said she was aiming for Pete. Well, that didn't help my throbbing temple. She offered to compensate me in the amount of $200. I agreed to meet her at Kmart. I took the money and promised to drop the police complaint. I knew I was capable of the same rash behavior if the circumstances were right.

The following weekend, I went to Chick's alone hoping to bump into Ronnie. He never came in that night. As I sat there, a guy walked in who I was not acquainted with. He came right over with a shit-eating grin on his face and asked if he could buy me a drink.

His name was Art Cronin. He was a short, bearded Irishman. He told me I looked like Adrienne Barbeau from the TV show Maude. I didn't tell him that he looked like a leprechaun. I didn't care that he found me attractive. All I was interested in that night was someone to buy my Dewar's, which he bought a lot of.

It was the end of November. Nobody wants to be alone for the holidays so I let Art think that he had a chance with me. He loved my kids and they adored him. He was funny and generous. He worked for the Scranton Times. He got them jobs delivering papers. He would even pick them up and drive them to their stops so they could get back in plenty of time for school.

Whenever the opportunity materialized, Ronnie and I were still having sex. I don't think the term "fuck buddies" had been coined yet but that was the best description for what we were doing. It was clandestine sex. Publicly I was Art's girlfriend.

One night, Art just showed up at my trailer with pizza. I had not invited him over. I was in no mood to fake affection. I belligerently stated I was upset because I didn't even have anything to drink. He gave me $20. I flew out the door and drove to the liquor store where I bought a bottle of Scotch.

Then I continued to the Nativity Club and ordered a

drink. That insufferable bartender Jerry was behind the bar. As I sipped my drink, I began to vent my frustration with men. Art was a saint with my kids but the idea of sex with him made my skin crawl. Ronnie on the other hand was good in bed but a confirmed bachelor.

With the wisdom of Solomon, Jerry opined, "You should marry Art and screw Ronnie on the side." I was very offended by his crude and unsolicited advice. I bought a six pack and returned home.

The end of November was my 20th High School reunion. I didn't want to bring Art but I didn't want to walk in alone. I had always stayed friendly with all my exes" families. Probably because the ex-husbands were such assholes. I imagined they saw me as saintlike for putting up with them as long as I did. I had graduated with Bob's sister Maryann Hoppel. I called her and she said she would be thrilled to go to the reunion with me.

I had nothing nice to wear. I browsed the Globe Store downtown to find something appropriate. I found this beautiful V cut emerald green sweater. At the time my hair was colored red. I knew that green sweater with my hazel eyes and crimson hair would make quite a statement. The price however was out of my league. I bought it anyway.

The night of the reunion, I tucked the price tag into my bra with intentions of returning it the next day.

I did get more than a few admiring looks the night of the Central High School Class of 1966 Reunion. I looked for my place card and found that I was at a table with all couples.

As I drank my scotch, who should approach me but that loudmouth from the Nativity Club. I asked him what he was doing there. He said, "I told you we went to high school together. We were in some of the same classes too."

When it was time for dinner, I noticed he was also sitting alone. When the dance music started, he asked me to dance. I was supposed to meet some friends of mine at Valentino's in Dickson City. I asked him if he wanted to go and have a drink with me. Of course, he said yes. I don't think I ever heard no to that question in my entire life.

We had fun dancing and drinking with my friends Debbie Williams and her sister. Debbie was Gary Williams ex. His apartment was where Ronnie and I had our first date. The population of Scranton might have been 80,000 but it was still a small-town environment.

About 2 AM we went to Tony Harding's for breakfast. There were three or four diners that stayed open for the drinking crowd. This diner was one of the most popular.

After our meal, Jerry walked me out to my car. We were both parked in Harding's back lot. I said I had a wonderful time and jumped in my car. I didn't give him time to kiss me. I had enough men in my life and, he was married.

Christmas Eve, I saw my parents, visited Aunt Gloria and cousins Larry, Jimmy and Paul Miller and had Christmas Dinner with Art's family. I had known one of Art's brothers when I was a teenager. They were delighted that Art was involved with me. Of course, they didn't know how expendable I felt he was.

New Year's Eve he celebrated with me and my friends at Valentino's in Dickson City. After midnight, the band played the song "Need you Now "by Lady Antebellum.

**"It's a quarter after one**

**I'm all alone and I need you now**

**Another shot of whisky**

**Can't stop looking at the door**

**Wishing you'd come sweeping in**

**the way you did before**

**And I wonder if I ever cross your mind**

**For me it happens all the time."**

I went to the pay phone and called Ronnie.

Happy New Year!

# CHAPTER 33

# THE SCOREBOARD

Here's a recap of 1986-1987 in case you are keeping score.

Jack fails to steal home base. Thrown out of the game with a second and final divorce. The jockey went back to Kentucky, so out at third base. Cousin Paul is still my drinking buddy and pinch hitter. Art the leprechaun is at first base and is very popular with my kids. Supposedly I struck out with Ronnie but we are still having sex. Jerry B. the bartender is waiting in the dugout, flirting, and lending me his ear whenever I feel like venting.

Valentine's Day, Art took me to a very romantic restaurant and after dinner proposed. The ring was quite beautiful so I accepted. It was a pragmatic decision on my part.

Realistically, none of my choices for the past 20 years had worked out. I had wanted to have a career as High School English teacher that was thwarted by my parents. I thought Jack Calvey was my soulmate (twice) and that proved to be an unsound perception. The urge to marry and have children resulted in the toxic imprisonment with Bob and the subsequent stalking when I tried to break free. Letting my guard down and being vulnerable with Ronnie Vaughn resulted ultimately in heartbreak.

I was growing weary and jaded. Maybe Jerry was right, marry Art and have Ronnie on the side. The only problem was that I never enjoyed cheating nor aspired to being the other woman. At heart, I was still that good Catholic girl that believed in the Ten Commandments. Although excommunicated by the Church due to divorce, still trying to play by their rules.

I was still stopping by the Nativity Club after work almost every day. The girls were 12- and 13-year-old latchkey kids. Jerry was trying to convince me that we could have a platonic relationship. How many plates could I keep spinning?

His friends repeatedly supported his case. They would tell me that his wife was a drapery drunk, slang for women who drank at home alone. I heard how the marriage was not a good one. However, calling his wife, a drunk was like the pot calling the kettle black.

St. Patrick's Day, I stopped in at Nativity as usual. I had

on my white nurses' uniform and a pin that said "Kiss My Irish Ass". Paul had met me for a drink although I did the buying as he was stone broke. The door opened and in came Jerry. He wasn't bartending today since he was Irish and therefore it was a sacred holy day. His full-time job was teaching Biology at Scranton Central High School, our alma mater. I told Paul he could leave. At least Jerry was able to pay for my drinks.

The girls were having a sleepover at a friend's house so I had no curfew. I don't remember much about that night but I do remember the next morning. I woke up to find Jerry in my bed. The girl's sleepover was at another mobile home in Honor Park so the girls could walk in at any time. I woke him and rushed him out the back door.

After breaking all my self-imposed rules, I decided I would see Jerry again. However, we would not sleep together. We would try his platonic approach.

The next day I stopped at Art's house unannounced, something I had never done before. After knocking loudly for more than a few minutes, I found that the door was unlocked. When I walked in, I discovered Art passed out drunk on the kitchen floor. I couldn't wake him up. He looked and smelled as if he had been on a drinking binge for a few days. I left feeling disgusted. My business-like decision to marry him became a nonstarter.

A few days later, I called him and asked him to meet me for an early dinner. We were sitting at a table in the middle of this very busy restaurant. The former Mayor of Scranton, Gene Peters came in. His entrance acquiring the room's full attention. A few minutes later, he stopped at our table and slipped me his phone number.

Attracting men had never been my problem. My problem was never attracting good men.

After our entrée, we ordered coffee. I told Art that it was not going to work out between us. He asked me if I was going to give him back the ring. I had purposely left the ring at home. I arrogantly replied, "A gentleman wouldn't ask for the ring back", as I threw my napkin at him and left the restaurant.

I had once again made a decision based upon "Situational Ethics". The justifying viewpoint being I still had to care of my children and the ring would buy a lot of groceries.

# CHAPTER 34

# PLATONIC RELATIONSHIP

I started seeing Jerry every Friday for dinner and drinks. He would pick me up at my trailer and we would go to some out of the way place. Our favorite was Nana's in Moosic. It was a family run Italian place. They kept the lights low and the Chianti flowing. We stayed platonic for a few weeks. Then we broke our nonphysical rule and became intimate. By the end of April, we were falling in love.

We would mail love letters to each other. I would mail his to the school. At the end of each letter, we would put a page number from 'Listen to The Warm" by Rod McKuen.

"Be gentle with me, new love

Treat me tenderly.

I need the gentle touch,

The soft voice,

The candlelight after nine.

There've been so many who didn't understand

So, give me all the love I see in your timid eyes but give it gently.

Please." Rod McKuen

Platonic had now gone to the other extreme. I could not take the ambivalent feelings I was experiencing. I was literally the other woman and I did not like it. I was not sleeping with Ronnie. I was not hanging out and drinking with Art or Paul. I had put all my eggs in one basket. A basket that had a very big hole in it. Situational ethics could not help me here.

The Roman Catholic Commandment Seven, "Thou shalt not commit adultery" persistently repeated in my brain. I felt like I was walking around with the Scarlet letter A on my forehead. My conscience could not rest. The Catholic girl was winning this fight.

The next time we had dinner I drove in my car to the lookout on Moosic Street. Couples went there to make out. If a cop knocked on your window you could say you were there for the beautiful nighttime view of the city below. The police would still tell you to move on but with a wink and a smile. The lookout was across the road from Lake

Scranton, a popular place for walking.

I had driven to this spot for a reason. I was ending something that should never have started in the first place. Jerry left his car in the Nativity parking lot. When we got to the romantic spot, I turned to him and said, "This will be the last night I see you." A look of disbelief and shock came over his face. He wanted to know what he did wrong. I told him that right from the beginning he kept pursuing me diligently even though he was married. I wouldn't go so far as to say he took advantage of me but his persistence did wear me down. I was not feeling good about being the other woman.

What happened next surprised me. He said "Is this really it?" I said yes and he started to cry. Manly tears of course. He opened the car door and commenced walking down Moosic Street. I slowly drove alongside him begging him to get back in the car. His stubborn Irish pride kept him from doing that.

I went home knowing that I had done the right thing. I now had experienced firsthand that there were educated nice men out there, much better than what I had chosen in the past. I had very deep feelings for Jerry. However, my self-esteem had been steadily growing this past year. I was not going to settle for being anyone's mistress.

The next morning Jerry called and asked me if he could meet me for breakfast. Terry's Diner was about three blocks from Honor Park. Thinking he needed closure I agreed. I drove into the diner parking lot prepared to stick to my guns. I got out of my car and he got out of his. He strode forcefully towards me. He grabbed me by the shoulders pushing his body against mine.

His face was close to mine when he asked, "Will you marry me"? To his surprise and mine, I responded "You will have to get divorced first."

# CHAPTER 35

# THE BRIER PATCH

Jerry's brother was a very prominent lawyer. John J. Brier rarely lost a case. He had worked in the District Attorney's office and private practice. He was such a good divorce lawyer that one man wanted to kill him. Attorney Brier had represented Linda Karabin in her divorce from Nicholas Karabin. Karabin told his girlfriend that he wanted to kill his wife, and told her that he intended to kill other people at random, so that his wife's murder would seem to be the work of a madman, and he would not be a suspect. He also had a hit list and Attorney Jack Brier was on it. Karabin was disturbed by the divorce proceedings which had been started by his wife and her attorney Jack Brier.

On March 17, 1978 Karabin told his girlfriend that he intended to begin the random murders that evening. After driving from Clarks Summit to Scranton with her in the car, Karabin drove to a location near the North Scranton Expressway, parked his car, announced that he intended to shoot someone on the expressway, and left the car, armed with a shotgun and wearing a disguise. She heard two shots and he returned to the car. He had killed a stranger.

He managed to kill two more people before his plan fell apart. He was caught before he could carry out the killings of those on his hit list. While incarcerated August 8, 1979, Nicholas Karabin, Jr. was found guilty by a jury of murder of Clarence Doolittle, a fellow inmate who was incarcerated at with him in the Lackawanna County Jail.

Jack Brier was also known for defending 16-year-old Joseph Aulisio, a high-profile murder case. Aulisio had killed his step brother and step sister. It took jurors one hour, 51 minutes to decide that Joseph G. Aulisio should die in the electric chair for the murders of Cheryl Ziemba, 8, and her brother, Christopher, The Old Forge youth remained expressionless as the court clerk read the verdict. Defense attorney Jack Brier clasped Aulisio's hand. Even the guilty need a lawyer and Jack had worked both sides of the aisle.

He had also represented my Ex, Bob every time there was a support hearing or he got caught in a small-time crime. When Bob heard that I divorced Jack (again), he called me. He must not have found out right away because usually he would jump on me the second, I was single. The funny thing was Jerry was sitting next to me when he called. When he started his spiel about still loving me, I interrupted him. I said. "Not only am I with someone but he is your lawyer's brother, so you need to find a new attorney too." Then I hung up and that was the last time I got a phone call from Mr. Harpo.

When Jerry told his brother, he wanted to start divorce proceedings, Jack Brier was a little surprised. They were both raised in an Irish Catholic family and no one got divorced. Like the Irish Catholic Cop played by Matt Damon in "The Departed". His character tells his psychoanalyst girlfriend that if their relationship is to end, she must be the one to break it off. His reason that being Irish, he never will. "I'm not capable," he says. "I'm fucking Irish. We just suffer and deal with something being wrong for the rest of our lives."

The first thing Attorney Brier told his brother to do was to move out of his house. He added that he couldn't move in with me. So, Jerry found a temporary roommate with one of his single friends.

Things were moving fast. In my heart, I believed in Jerry fully. He was just an inherently good person. He was a much better person than I. But I had trusted before and been betrayed. I had always used the coping methods of alcohol and/or sex to deal with unwanted feelings. Feeling uncertain, insecure, and after having a few drinks one night, I found myself knocking on Ronnie's door. He let me in and offered me a drink. In all the times, I had randomly showed up, I never found him with another woman. He excused himself to go the bathroom.

I called the Nativity Club and told Jerry I'd be late. As I hung up, Ronnie came out of the bathroom buck naked. I think that was the moment I knew that I really did love Jerry. I got up and told Ronnie "If I'm going to make it with Jerry, I can't do this with you anymore". I quickly ran down the steps to the street and drove directly to the club.

I was not going to be the one to endanger what we had. Quite the contrary. At that moment, I made myself a vow. I swore in my heart that I would do whatever I had to do to insure we would stay together.

A few days later, Lady Fate made an appearance in the form of my mailman. I was getting my mail and started a conversation with my mailman Jonesy. He had been one of my customers when I owned My Place. As we were chatting, I mentioned that I would like to own a bar again. My reasoning being I would have an equal partner this time and it would be a dream come true for Jerry.

The mailman said he knew of a bar in South Side that was

thinking of selling. The Locust Inn wasn't on the market yet. I went the next day to talk to the owner. The man, Carl, had the business for years but he was old and tired. I told him my background in the bar business and that I had the connections to make it happen. We struck a deal. I told him, I would get contracts drawn up and be back in a few days. Even with my experience and contacts, I would still need resources from Jerry. I already had vendors in mind to help with the purchase Jimmy Judge and Ray Petritus.

Next, I took my plan, all neatly packaged to Jerry. With the vendors investment and the sale of my mobile home, we might be able to pull it off. We conferred with our lawyer who said since Jerry had left the family home and filed for divorce, it would not be considered in the divorce settlement.

Negotiating this deal was a real Catch 22. The vendors would loan us $15,000 after the bank approved our loan. Jerry's parents loaned him $15,000 with the understanding that as soon as the bank loan went through, he would pay them back. Then he went to a bank and brokered a loan. The loan was approved. Ray and Jim gave us the $15,000 to repay his parents. We then paid the vendors monthly from the poker machine income. Of course, my name could not be on any of the paper work or the deed. This I didn't like but I felt strongly enough about Jerry to make a leap of faith.

My trailer sold almost immediately. The current owners of the bar agreed to store some of my furniture till the sale went through.

While we waited for the closing, Jerry rented a cabin at Chapmans Lake for me and the girls. It was June and school was out for the summer. I was not working because of a recent car accident. It was like taking a long vacation. Paul would come and stay over sometimes since Jerry had to maintain a morally correct façade. Once again, I had a bodyguard but this one, I would not sleep with. Paul and I would drink and smoke pot and exchange stories from the "old days". Jerry felt more at ease about my safety with him there at night.

By August, we could move in to the East Locust Street property. It was not just a bar but also had several apartments to rent. Across the street lived my chiropractor, Dr. Bob. We had been drinking buddies in the past. He was a lot younger than me and our relationship was genuinely nonsexual. The fact that Jerry and I had both grown up in South Side just made the bar's location seem so perfect. We knew everyone in South Scranton and were sure we'd have an ample customer base.

Our living quarters were a little cramped at first. Jerry had to pretend to live in one of the upstairs apartments until his divorce was final. His family did not know at first that he was filing for divorce. They thought it was a trial separation. His Irish Catholic family took the Ten Commandments very seriously. At least, overtly. I'm sure the Brier boys broke a lot of the commandments  but not openly. My involvement in the bar was explained away as a business partner.

The next three months everything was great. I was good at the money and management of the business. I worked the day shift and Jerry did the night shift. We had plans to remodel and have a larger living space.

But Lady Luck could be a fickle mistress, as one night in November spectacularly demonstrated.

# CHAPTER 36

# WALL OF FLAMES

November 30 1987 at 5 A.M. we were awakened by our fire alarm and what sounded like "pops". Half asleep, we first thought it was an intruder. Jerry jumped up and grabbed the baseball bat he kept next to the bed. As he neared the door that connected our residence with the bar, he could feel the heat. Our dream was on fire.

We woke the kids and pushed them towards the back door. My youngest daughter wouldn't leave without our dog. Mariah, a miniature Irish Red Setter who was a rescue dog before that was a thing. Jerry picked the dog up and carried her out. My daughters and I headed out through the kitchen back door.

Flames were shooting out of the first-floor window of the bar side of the building. The girls and I sat on Dr. Bob's porch. Jerry ran back and up the stairs to the second floor to wake up one of our tenants, George Kavulich. The other tenant a young bartender named Jack McCawley was able to climb down the second-floor railing and jump to safety.

The next day The Scranton Times ran a picture of the building ablaze. They reported that the Arson Investigator, Tim Lavelle said the blaze apparently started in the bar. The investigation into the cause could not begin because the second floor, weakened by the fire damage, collapsed into the first floor. He also reported some six inches of water must be drained from the ruins before a full-scale probe could be launched into the cause.

Our dream laid in ruins but we still had each other. The girls went to my parents' home and The Red Cross put us up at the Holiday Inn. The fire and resulting headlines also put our relationship in the spotlight. Exposed was the true nature of our relationship as more than business partners.

Jerry's parents and soon to be ex-wife may have suspected that we were romantically involved. Now they knew for sure that it was so. Our secret completely out, we were relieved. We rented an apartment while we tried to rebuild Marie's Brier Patch.

I was also relieved when the insurance adjuster who showed up was someone from my past. Frank Jenkins was someone who I had briefly worked for and the adjuster on the fire when I was with Bob. I let out a sigh of relief and told Jerry, we'd be okay. Nationwide paid 90% of what we ultimately spent on the reconstruction and remodeling.

As soon as we got clearance, Jerry would go over every day and help the workers that cleaned up the burnt wood, broken glass and all the resulting fire and smoke damage. He would come home after dark and be covered in soot. I would draw him a bath and scrub him clean, as he wept.

The average time to rebuild after a fire can range from several weeks to several months, so we had to be patient. We had to replace sheetrock, restore fire-damaged floors and electrical wiring.

As a family we also were experiencing several stages of adjustment. Jerry and I both dealing with shock, anger, depression, and hopelessness. The girls, now teenagers, were showing some telltale signs of angst.

The rainbow after the storm was that we could now get a jump on the remodeling we had planned. Gone would be the cramped living quarters. We now would have the second and third floor on the left side of the building for family. The entire first floor would be a bar and restaurant. Tenants would live on the upper right side of the building.

Positive feelings begin to re-emerge as the focus shifted once again towards the future. Life was moving forward once again.

# CHAPTER 37

# SAMSKARAS

I believe that my abandonment issues existed at a cellular level. I think that when my mother made the premeditated decision to miscarry, the seed of unworthiness was planted.

The Buddhists believe that there are energy patterns that get stuck in your heart and block your energy flow. Many Indian religions call them Samskaras. My feelings of fear, anxiety, unworthiness, and hopelessness literally started in the womb. I tried to push those feelings down. First with overachieving and trying to fix everyone's problems. Later by self-medicating with alcohol , food and men.

Christmas Eve 1987 those Samskaras were about to be triggered once again. Jerry's family was not ready to accept my existence or his divorce proceedings.

His very large family had the holiday tradition of everyone getting together on Christmas Eve. Usually 50 or more Briers under one roof. He promised me he would just make an appearance and then return to home to me. After two hours my anger started to escalate. No cell phones then or I would have been relentlessly texting him.

By the time he finally called me my slow burn had turned into a full boil. He told me that his parents had invited his soon to be ex Jeanne. That was to be expected since his two children were in the mix. Then he told me she was wearing makeup and dressed very nicely. I told him he better be back at our apartment in ten fucking minutes. In retrospect, I would have done the same thing if I was her.

By the time he got home, all my stored negative energy exploded. My inner cynic had reared her pessimistic head. The abandoned little girl was confused and angry. My slightly drunk man didn't have a chance in this fight. He said all the things men say when they are blatantly wrong. I'm sorry, I didn't know she would be there, I love you, etc.

Then he held my hand and gave me my Christmas present. It was a tiny box. That was a good sign. I started to calm down. I unwrapped it and there was a little black velvet box. I held my breath and opened it.

What I discovered was a stud earring with a medium size diamond. I incredulously asked him, "What's this". He replied "It's the diamond that I bought for your engagement ring. Until we can be officially engaged, I thought you could wear it as an earring." I just flew into a rage. After throwing the ring box in his face, I said, "You wear it in your ear, you son of a bitch."

I was used to men disappointing me. I hoped that my instinct to trust Jerry wasn't a mistake. I had literally given him everything. My home, my heart, my children's future, our very survival as a family unit were all in his hands.

That wasn't our best Christmas. However, the following day Jerry called his parents. He told them he was creating a new family. One that included his children but also me and my children. He told them that from now on if I was not welcomed then neither was, he. That elevated my trust level back up a few points. It still was not at 100% but I trusted him more than any other man from my past involvements.

Valentine's Day, the little gift box he gave me contained the engagement ring that sanctioned our romantic union and marital future. Easter arrived and his mother called and invited us all up to the country. We had won one battle but not the war. His sister Annmarie told me she would never accept me because of her strong Catholic beliefs. His sister-in-law Millie would leave the room whenever I entered. His parents tried to be warm but I could feel the undercurrent of judgment.

The Brier kids were wonderful and welcomed their new cousins with gusto. They all went outside to play volleyball. After dinner and more than a few drinks, the adults were ready to play. They pulled out green T-shirts that read either in-law or out-law and put them on to designate which side of the net they were playing on.

I was glad I did not wear my engagement ring to that family gathering. I wasn't sure if I was going to be an in-law or and outlaw.

# CHAPTER 38

# RELENTLESS RIVALS

The year started with me taking on two missions. I decided that this was the perfect time to finish my college degree at the University of Scranton. We were still not married which meant my financial aid would cover the cost.

The other undertaking would be to supervise the rebuilding of Marie's Brier Patch. I was the quasi contractor. I planned the layout and restoration we wanted for our new business and living quarters. I would be on site when I wasn't in class. I would go to the plumbing, wood, and other building material suppliers with the orders for supplies.

We had a legal official contractor that made sure everything was up to code, apply for any necessary permits and made sure we were adhering to building codes.

I really enjoyed my new power buying the fixtures and building supplies. I would go into the plumbing store for instance and the salesman would ignore me at first. When he finally approached and said "What can I do for you today, little lady?" I would reply I need eight toilets, six-bathroom sinks, four shower stalls and a jacuzzi to start. The look on his face told me he was absolutely flabbergasted.

My choices were not always practical. The jacuzzi was for our master bath which was on the third floor. They needed a crane to hoist it up there.

Practical or not we got it down in a little over three months. We had shuffle board, a pool table, vending machines and a separate room for dining. I kept the menu simple, steak or fettucine in clam sauce, cheeseburgers, and pizza.

We ran an ad in the Scranton Times for the Grand Re-Opening of "Marie's Brier Patch". The entertainment was Jimmy Tigue, one of my old flames. The place was filled to the rafters and confirmed our copacetic natures for this type of business. Fueled with ambition and love, we built a successful enterprise.

The St. Patrick's Parade Day in Scranton is one of the largest Saint Patrick's Day parades in the United States. It is held in Scranton, Pennsylvania every year on the Saturday of the weekend before St. Patrick's Day.

Each year, thousands of people line the streets of downtown Scranton on Parade Day to take part in one of the city's greatest traditions. The city has hosted a St. Patrick's Day Parade since early in its history, with the current iteration being held annually since 1862. The Parade is sponsored and organized by the St. Patrick's Day Parade Association of Lackawanna County.

I would make lots of ham and cabbage. We would put green beer on tap for that day. After the parade, our bar would be filled with partiers. Irish just for the day. That was the biggest money maker every year.

We never missed an opportunity for an event. We had wet t-shirt contests using a kiddie pool. We formed a billiards team and joined the NE Pennsylvania Pool League. We also had a coed soft ball team.

For these events the team members had dark green shirts with Marie's Brier Patch in white and a single rose. We also had jackets and hats made. We joined the Lackawanna County Tavern Association.

Our Halloween parties were epic. We gave prizes for best costumes. The first year we dressed as Herman and Lily Munster and stayed in character all night.

We did fishing trips, golf trips, anything, and everything to get our name out there. We had the atmosphere of the TV show "Cheers". A place where everyone knows your name and your drink order, where you feel like family. Customers want to know they can get a shot and a beer, with top shelf alcohol and beer on tap, a cocktail, or a glass of wine. People want a place where they can go to relax, connect with friends, be treated well by the bartender.

Unfortunately, in South Scranton there was a bar on every corner. We had a lot of competition. But our bar was a clear reflection of the neighborhood and who we were. We had a very loyal clientele.

My friends Joanie and Renie, and my sister Ann bartended when I had class. Jerry usually took over after school but that was getting to be too much to do every day.

Joanie had a friend named Coz who she recommended to bartend. His real name was Jimmy McCormick but everyone called him Coz. When we knew that it would be busier than usual, we also had two back up bartenders that doubled as bouncers, Joe Costanzi, and Mike Novak. There were a few occasions that they jumped over the bar to break up a fight.

The funniest situation was when an old boyfriend would come in. Ronnie, Art, Roger, among a few. Jack even pulled his truck up outside but didn't have the guts to come in. My friend Vernon stopped in one day, toothpick hanging out of his mouth. He was so happy for me.

Jerry's self-worth wasn't threatened in the least by the parade of exes. After a few drinks there might be some macho one-up-Manship. One night Ronnie and Jerry started a battle of words. It was my birthday and Jerry had given me opal and diamond earrings. Ronnie yelled down the bar, "Well, I gave her opal earrings on her birthday last year". Jerry won the debate by saying "But whose ring is on her finger?"

There was one guy named Ed that I never went out with, even though he had asked several times. He would get drunk and start making obnoxious remarks. Jerry threw him out on two separate occasions. The third time, it was a hot summer night and we had just the screen door that night. Jerry had already told him that he was "barred" {banned}.

We didn't serve him but he was already drunk when he walked in. That was the worst when someone would get kicked out from a bar down the street and then show up at ours. When he wouldn't leave, Jerry picked him up by the pants and threw him out. The problem was that he didn't take the time to open the door. Ed went right through the screen. We needed to buy a new screen door but the excruciatingly obnoxious Ed never came back.

**"In love there are no friends anywhere. Where there is a pretty woman, hostility is open."**

**Victor Hugo,** " Les Misérables"

# CHAPTER 39

# PONCHO AND THE RABBIT

We had a cast of characters worthy of a Tarantino movie. Poncho who ran a roofing crew, a swarthy Latino guy who carried a certain air of danger. I knew him for years. Jack even worked for him. He was always very protective of me. When I was going to bars alone, if he was there, he would keep an eye on me.

He had a quiet demeanor, never raised his voice, but when he spoke you listened. He and a couple of his cohorts liked to make the rounds on rainy Saturdays when they couldn't work. They would start early at Tony and Mary's or the Sun Hotel, bars who opened at the crack of dawn. There were a few other bars on their itinerary. They spent a lot of money but you prayed you were at the top of the list not further down.

In this group were Pete Dubiac and Lennie Marullo , both of whom I had known since a teenager. The fourth member had the nickname Rabbit. His real name was Michael Dunnigan. Rabbit was extremely intelligent and well read. When sober he was downright charming.

He would start off with some erudite conversation. Then he would get change from me for the Juke Box. We were known for having the Oldies from the fifties and sixties. He would often play the same tunes, such as "I Heard it from the Grapevine.". He was quite tall with very long legs. After more than a few drinks, he would start to dance. He would look like a flamingo on crack.

An African American woman used to come in on those rainy days too. Everyone called her Black Mary. I guess to differentiate from the white Mary's. Rabbit would love to dance with her. She would love the drinks he would buy her.

One of these rainy Saturdays, I was feeling a little stressed. Rabbit was quite drunk and very annoying. They all wanted cheeseburgers. I made sure everyone had a drink and then went into the kitchen and turned on the grill. Unfortunately, Rabbit thought I wanted company. I told him nicely to get out. Then I told him firmly to get out.

We had a commercial refrigerator with glass doors. We bought it second hand and I had assumed it was double paned. Finally, I lost my temper and yelled at him to get out.

For added emphasis I slammed my hand on the glass door of the cooler. To my surprise my hand went right through it.

Now I was beyond stressed out. My wrist was bleeding profusely. Poncho came into the kitchen and wrapped a kitchen towel around it. I went out to the bar and told Joanie to bartend.

I then looked around and evaluated who was the most sober of the gang. Lennie Marullo didn't seem legally drunk yet, so I had him drive me to the emergency room. I needed stitches. I still have the two-inch scar on my right wrist. Matching the (self-harm) scar on my left wrist from a few years back.

When Jerry got home, Rabbit told him that I had cut my wrist and was at the emergency room. When my love got there, he treated me very coldly. Finally, I asked him what the hell the attitude was about. The way Rabbit told him what happened, he thought it was a suicide attempt. When he heard the real story, he felt like a fool and couldn't apologize enough.

Rabbit was barred. Being barred from the Brier Patch at the time was a cruel punishment. That's where the action was. He tried to beguile me with balloons and flowers. After two weeks, I gave in.

When Jerry and I worked together for special events, we would of course be drinking. We also had different styles of bartending. I used a shot glass for mixed drinks. He liked to free-pour. This irritated my business sense to no end. At least he was charging for the drinks unlike Jack.

After we both had a few drinks, he would really start to annoy me. He would do things that he knew would irritate me. I would get angry. When I reached my limit, I would throw an ashtray at him. My aim was quite good and I aimed to just miss him. The patrons loved it. The Friday night fights at the Brier Patch and you didn't even need Pay-Per-View.

The other area where we differed on was closing time. Closing time in Pennsylvania was 2 AM. He would lock the door at 2 AM but if you were still in the bar, he would keep serving drinks. I gave up trying to win this one. Instead, I would just go to bed. However, one night, it was 3 AM and the music was blaring. The juke box was so loud that it was keeping me awake.

I went downstairs in my pajamas and proceeded to throw everyone out, including Jerry. A little while later I heard activity again. Jerry was back and trying to let people back in. This time I called the police. Before they got there,

Jerry went out the back door. He was quite drunk but I still did not entertain the idea that either of us was alcoholic.

I would also flirt with guys if I was mad at him. I loved when the ex-boyfriends would come in. Especially Ronnie. There was a neighbor named Victor that was a policeman. He was ruggedly handsome in that Italian way. One night after an argument with Jerry, I left with him and went to an after-hours place called Bella's. Jerry was still behind the bar.

We had no sooner ordered a drink than there was Jerry staring at us at the end of the bar at Bella's. Obviously, he got somebody to take his place at our bar. I apologized to Victor and drove Jerry home.

We did a brisk takeout business too. Take out was supposed to be just supposed to be beer. Except for my friend Dr. Bob. He would call me for drinks to go. It was the middle of the day and he would be seeing patients. He would tell me to be creative but make sure it packed a wallop. I would run the drink across the street. Everyone thought he was the best chiropractor ever to practice. I went to him even knowing he drank while he was working. Everyone knew. He was a genius at spinal adjustments.

Jerry fell off a ladder one Sunday and crawled into the

bar. Dr. Bob came right over and within two minutes, Jerry was standing with no pain.

Many great men and women have had prolific lives despite their addictions. Winston Churchill is the face of World War II in England. He was notorious for drinking whisky. He also took amphetamines repeatedly to be able to stay up and plan the war. His resilience inspired many, but he paid for it with his health.

Dr. Bob was the best chiropractor I had ever seen but one day he would pay a great price for his drug and alcohol addictions.

# CHAPTER 40

# SHAME & SCANDAL

Jerry's divorce finally came through. The first thing I asked him was if his brother had my name added to the deed. When we bought the place, I couldn't be listed as the divorce was not final. There was a lot of juggling and compartmentalizing assets. He told me of course your name is now on the deed.

The next day I went downtown to the County Courthouse. I walked into the office of the County Recorder of Deeds. I asked to look at 639 E Locust Street. My heart was racing as I waited for the clerk to locate the record. I could not take another betrayal of trust. When I finally saw it, there was my name as co-owner. I let out a sigh.

The next thing on my agenda was for us to get married. I was turning 41 in October and I wasn't going to wait any longer than I had to. Jerry's family grudgingly were starting to accept me. However, once we were legally married, I thought that should warm  their hearts a little.

My father almost threw a monkey wrench into my dream wedding plans. I always felt my father wasn't totally straight. He would bring home men and they would drink in the basement all night. I remember two that were there frequently. He made many trips to New York City without my mom. Add to those details that they were not affectionate to each other.

I got the call from my mother that we needed a family meeting. I just remember Joe and I being there. Two of our male second cousins had accused my father of inappropriate behavior.It was alleged that he would have them watch male porno movies and then touch them.

The decision was made to see a good lawyer, Attorney Thomas Munley. The very lawyer that had represented me pro bono in Jessup. Ultimately, because it was family and no one wanted it in the newspaper, a settlement was reached. $5,000 for each boy.

The following week my father tried to kill himself in his closed garage with the car motor running. My mother and sister found him and called 911. He was revived and taken to the Veterans Hospital in Wilkes-Barre.

My father had a dark, confused soul. I couldnt begin to understand this latest behavior. Had something happened to him, the four years he spent in St. Joseph's orphange? Had my father been sexually abused? Was it a case of suppressed sexual orientation?

Those are questions that I cannot answer.

The events of that year were never spoken of again.

# CHAPTER 41

# CIVIL CEREMONY

Jerry was playing golf with his dad and mentioned that we were planning a civil wedding at first. When his annulment went through, we would then marry in church. His father got his hackles up and piously informed his son that would not be possible. The Catholic church was not going to annul a marriage that had produced two children.

Jerry explained to him that I had my marriage to Jack annulled and then received "A Dissolution Non-Forma" for my divorce from Bob. I was a Catholic in good standing because I filled out the paperwork and paid the tariff.

In the Catholic church an annulment, is a judgment made by a Tribunal of the Catholic Church that based on evidentiary proof a given relationship was not a binding marriage in the way the Catholic Church understands marriage to have been established by Almighty God.

The one important qualifier for annulment was if it had not been committed in good faith. Jerry had to testify that he got married because he wanted children but was not necessarily in love with his wife. I am sure he did love Jean. The problem with marrying young is you really don't understand what committed love means.

Jerry had to prove that one of the essential elements of marriage or the necessary personal capacity for competent consent was lacking at the time the he wed. A relationship which may have approximated marriage according to civil or social standards is deemed not to have been a binding marriage in the way marriage was ordained by Almighty God. Whew! It sounds more complicated than it was.

Meantime, our civil wedding could be planned. We decided to get married at Lake Scranton. There was a stone platform with steps leading up to a spectacular view of the lake. My maid of honor was Joan of course. My daughters Trina and Traci were bridesmaids. Jerry's longtime friend Gene Raymond was his best man. Mike Brier and Michael Dunnigan (Rabbit) were groomsmen.

Ironically, my father had disappeared since his attempted suicide and subsequent trip to the VA. My mother claimed no knowledge of his whereabouts. Mike Novak escorted me up the steps and to my waiting fiancé in lieu of my father.

We married on a very cold and windy day in November. I was picked up in a 1954 Candy Apple red Ford by Jimmy Morell. He was a collector of vintage cars and a good friend of Jerry's.

I wore a long white dress, flowers in my hair and a faux mink stole. Thankfully it was a short ceremony. Magistrate Russell pronounced us man and wife and Jerry pretended to jump into the lake.

First, we had to stop at the Nativity Club where it all started. We walked in with our wedding party and ordered drinks.

Then driving through South Side, horns blaring, triumphantly arriving at Marie's Brier Patch.

I told Renie who was bartending to keep playing a certain song on the jukebox. I wanted it to be playing when we walked in. We made our entrance to the song "Going to The Chapel of Love "by The Dixie Cups.

Jerry's whole family was there. Also, friends and customers. My Capitol Records girlfriends were all there except for Priscilla. Our beautiful, funny sweet Priscilla had died in July. She was only 41.

I had finally picked a good man. I was feeling elated

and content. My life was finally going to be good. But I also knew how unpredictable life could be. I prayed no more roadblocks would deter me. I prayed that I finally had reached the mountain top, rock, and all.

"Mann Tracht, Un Gott Lacht" is an old Yiddish adage meaning, "Man Plans, and God Laughs."God was already chuckling.

# CHAPTER 42

# SEA OF LOVE

We had planned on leaving from the reception straight to the honeymoon. Our plane was leaving from Avoca Airport in thirty minutes and my husband could hardly stand up. I had drunk quite a bit but as usual seemed sober as a judge.

I sternly warned Jerry to keep his mouth shut till the plane took off. I told him if they knew he was drunk we might not be allowed on the flight. He pouted but remained quiet till we got to our honeymoon destination.

We landed in Orlando, Florida and I checked us into our hotel. Once in our room, he promptly passed out. I ordered a movie from the hotel's pay per view.

I spent my wedding night watching Jodie Foster in "The Accused". Based on a true story about rape and the objectification of the female in a patriarchal society. Perfect wedding night viewing.

The next morning, we left on the Princess Cruise Line

for the Bahamas. It was the first cruise for both of us. The seas were a little rough. I must have sailor blood because I stayed upright and did not get seasick. Jerry was not so lucky.

They seated us at a group table with two other couples. The Cohens and the Steins. Mrs. Cohen was the table interrogator. She asked us a million questions and seemed overly interested in my marital history.

The food was great and the entertainment fabulous. The next morning, we docked at Green Turtle Cay, part of the Abacos Islands. Named for the many green turtles found in the area. It was also known for its charming colonial architecture. The public dock serves as an official Port of Entry to the Abacos.

We were swimming in the Caribbean Sea on a beautiful sundrenched day. As newlyweds are prone to do, we were getting intimate underwater. It's amazing the ways you can have sex when you are young and flexible. For some reason, we were the only ones in the water.

Suddenly, I heard someone calling my name. It was the inquisitive Mrs. Cohen. We just waved and continued what we were doing. Of course, we were giggling thinking how shocked she would be if she knew what we were up to. The rest of the cruise we could not look at her without laughing.

The next day the cruise ship left for Cape Canaveral where we disembarked. Cape Canaveral (Spanish: Cabo Canaveral) is a prominent cape in Brevard County, Florida. When we were teens, it was called Cape Kennedy from 1963 to 1973. Then they changed the name to Cape Canaveral. It is part of a region known as the Space Coast. Port Canaveral, is one of the busiest cruise ports in the world. We visited the Cape Canaveral Lighthouse and of course the space center.

Our next part of the trip was Disney World, where we spent two days. My favorite park was Epcot. Especially the World Showcase that encompassed 11 pavilions representing countries from around the world, including the U.S.A, U.K., Japan, Morocco, France, Canada, Mexico, China, Norway, Germany, and Italy. Each pavilion had dining, drinking, and shopping relating to the country. We drank in every country.

We flew home and landed in the Scranton-Wilkes Barre Airport. We decided we needed a day to decompress before heading back to the madness of the Brier Patch. We took a cab to the Woodlands Resort and stayed the night.

Reality could wait one more day.

# CHAPTER 43

# AUDACIOUS ACTS

I was doing inventory when the phone rang. It was my father. He said, "Mom tells me you think she killed me and buried me in the back yard." Always the joker. I guess that's where I get my sense of humor from. He then confessed he had been in rehab and then sober living. He was coming home the next day. We finally had one member of the family who admitted they were an alcoholic.

June 1990, I graduated from the University of Scranton with a B.S. in Health and Human Services. Both my mother and father were there to see me get my diploma. There was a feeling of validation and triumph. Despite the lack of support from my parents, I  had attained another goal on Maslow's hierarchy.

Jerry and I fell back into the routine of running the bar. Jerry had his teaching job at Central High School and I was running the bar fulltime. So, our lives were quite hectic. We also had two teenage girls to contend with.

Jerry's daughter had turned 13 and we were told that

she was misbehaving. She had always been Daddy's girl so the divorce was a difficult adjustment. We met with Jean to discuss how we could help. I got along with Jean from the minute I met her.

The first time we met was summer 1987 at the Nativity Church Picnic. I spotted her when she arrived. When she saw me, she turned and started to leave. I ran after her. I told her that I always wanted our interactions to be civil for the sake of the children. I think she appreciated my candor.

So, three years later, as we sat in the living room discussing the usual problems you have with a 13-year girl. It was quite amicable. I had one of those impulsive moments of speaking before thinking. I asked if she would like to have the girl come live with us? To our surprise she said that might work.

Now there were three teenage girls living under our roof. Luckily the two younger ones bonded immediately.

It was deer season and Jerry and his brothers had a cabin they liked to use. They would go for the weekend. I had eaten venison before. Occasionally Jack or one of his friends would shoot a deer. I was looking forward to making some venison chili. I just made sure I had extra help in the bar on Friday and Saturday night.

We were quite busy that weekend. After last call and cleaning up, I did not get to bed till after 3 AM. I was awakened shortly after that by yelling and screaming outside. I went to the second-floor porch to see what was going on. One of my tenants and his girlfriend were being held at gunpoint by another man.

I yelled, “Hey what’s going on?” The gunman turned the gun toward me and told me to mind my own business. I backed into the house and called the police. I felt no fear for myself but I did have three young girls in my care. I was relieved to hear sirens, almost immediately.

I recognized the man with the gun so I filled out a police report. Within days I was approached by some regular customers who were his friends asking me to drop the charges. They said he was a great guy and just having woman trouble. They also said he was willing to pay me $500.

As a business person, I wanted to keep the goodwill of my customers. Therefore, I took the money and dropped the charges.

There was one other time a crime was thwarted while my husband was away. I heard noises coming from the alley side of the building. Again, I went out on that second floor and saw a known addict, Bozo Brennan trying to open a window into the bar.

I yelled "Hey Bozo. I know who you are so you better get out of here".

He ran. I called the police. They said I should have let him break in and then called them. They couldn't arrest him for trying to open a window. Right, I'm going to let a guy break in with three girls in the house and my husband out of town.

This was South Side. You knew everyone. You knew who the drug addicts and petty thieves were. Most times you could settle things without police but it was a thin line to be walked. I had many instances of this sort at my first bar.

When I had the bar in Throop a regular customer was selling me hamburger patties dirt cheap. I didn't ask questions. The saying was "It fell off the truck". I had bought kegs of beer and steaks on that premise.

However, I found out the guy selling me the burgers was stealing them from his parents. They had a small restaurant down the street. As soon as I found that out, I told him I was done.

A short time later, his parents were found murdered in the apartment above their restaurant in Throop. Rumor was the son had a bad drug habit and that some of his hoodlum friends were involved. The eighties were a perilous time to say the least.

I felt safe in our building in 1990. I had tenants that would be there for me in a second. Also, Jerry stopped taking trips that left me at home alone.

One of those tenants was our bartender Coz. He was a terrific bartender and would do anything for us. He started to date my friend Joan. Dating meaning sitting at our bar and drinking every night. She ended up moving in with him.

They were a typical alcoholic couple. Joan had tried rehab in 1981. The Scranton State Hospital had one of the first treatment programs in the area . But a short time after leaving that program, she relapsed. She went back to drinking. Alcoholism is sometimes a family affair. Her mother and father had both died from alcohol related disease.

Coz knew he was an alcoholic but didn't care. He would drink and then go out and throw up blood. He would come back in and order another beer. Joan and Coz were 10 years younger than Jerry and I . We became quite close and did everything together.

We went on mini vacations with them. Joan and I

would hold our breath and hope we weren't going to get kicked out of the restaurant or hotel. We did get kicked out of the jacuzzi area once, but it was merited.

Jerry would call them "the kids" but he was the biggest kid of all.

# CHAPTER 44

# BLACKOUT

Our dog Mariah had died and we got an orange tabby cat and named him the Muffin Man. He was loving and sweet to us but not everyone else was so lucky. We had been going to Florida for two weeks every winter. We would take him in a cat carrier.

Parts of Route 81 south can be very dangerous in the winter. It had been snowing and sleeting on this trip. Suddenly, a car far ahead of us went into a spin. It caused a domino effect. Soon there were at least 50 cars involved. Jerry ended up off the road facing a mountainside. He got out of the car to assess the situation. I was facing the mountain and could not see what was happening. An 18-wheeler lost control and landed on our car. All the windows imploded and I instinctively went into a crash position. They finally got us out of the car. I saw the cab of the truck was on top of our car and realized I could have been killed. I was taken to a hospital to be checked out. I seemed ok and checked into a hotel to wait for Jerry. He had to get the car towed and the cat was with him.

When he got to the hotel, he let Muffin out of his carrier. To our dismay and surprise, it was filled with broken glass. There was not a scratch on Muffin. I guess we both had nine lives. The car was totaled. Jerry's brother Jack came the next day to return us home.

We bought a brand-new Subaru Legacy. We always liked Subaru because of how it handled in the snow.

After this last car accident, I started to have spasms in my back. I went to see an orthopedist. Dr. Pelicci prescribed pain meds and muscle relaxers. This turned out to be a big problem. On both bottles it said "Do Not Take with Alcohol".

I decided that cautionary advice did not apply to me. I wasn't the ordinary person who had one or two drinks on the weekend. I had a very high tolerance for alcohol .But I thought it might be a slight problem.  I came up with a solution. I told my regular bartender, Coz, I was only going to have one drink every night.

Unlike Alice in Wonderland, I would swallow my pills big or small with alcohol. A Southern Comfort Manhattan in one of our oversize brandy snifters. Then I could sip on that and be sociable with my customers.

The very first night Coz made me a delicious Manhattan as planned. I was having wonderful conversations and enjoying people watching. Sooner than expected, my snifter was empty. I pushed it forward and waited for it to be refilled. After a few minutes, I beckoned Coz over. I asked him to please give me a refill. He bent forward and whispered, “But you told me to give you just one.” I know I replied but I’m fine.

Something began that night that never happened in twenty years of drinking. I started having blackouts. People would tell me things I did the night before and I would have no memory of it. For someone who likes to be in control that was frightening.

I also became very depressed, No one knew I was depressed. I was a good actress. But every morning I woke up with dark thoughts. I didn’t want to die but I didn’t want to live either. A morbid incongruity.

I decided a shopping trip might cheer me up. I went to the Wilkes Barre Mall. I was coming home on Route 81, when something happened that would send me down yet another road in my journey. I felt my left-hand jerk and next thing I knew I was in a tail spin. I hit every side of my car on the guard rails before I came to a full stop. It's a miracle that I didn't veer into a path of a truck and been killed. My guardian angel was in charge that day. I drove away from the scene with no bodily injuries.

If a cat has nine lives than I must be a different kind of animal. I was well past nine lives at this point..

I won't go into the consternation my husband exhibited or the shock of family and friends.

I was unraveling. A few days later, I took the car to Maaco to get an estimate. It was totaled. I drove home feeling totally vanquished.

After I parked, I said aloud, "God please help me, I can't take this anymore!" I immediately thought of Dr. Bob and the place he went to when things got out of control for him. I walked into his office and before the end of the day, my journey in life took a 180 degree turning point.

# CHAPTER 45

# DENIAL AND DETOX

As we drove up the road to Marworth Treatment Center, I felt relieved. A relaxing stress-free week at a spa might be just what I needed. Imagine my surprise when they went through my luggage and took my magazines and bathing suit. They told me I would not be needing those things.

Marworth served from 1931 to 1981 as the family estate for three generations of the Scranton family. The estate name is derived from the first names of Margery and Worthington Scranton, parents of former Pennsylvania Governor William Scranton.

In 1982, after a generous donation from the Scranton family, Marworth Alcohol & Chemical Dependency Treatment Center officially opened. The original 22,000-sq.-ft. building was expanded to better serve the individuals seeking recovery from drug or alcohol addiction.

I was told there would be a medical detoxification, or

medical detox. Alcohol withdrawal is life-threatening when severe, medical alcohol detox is an absolute necessity. I was given Librium, a benzodiazepine that helps to control the anxiety symptoms of alcohol detoxification. The first week is a blur. They call it the "Librium Shuffle".

The action of Librium on the brain to produce the GABA neurotransmitter assists with regulating anxiety and panic symptoms, and controls confused thinking. In the right doses and with the right supervision, Librium also relieves tremors. I think it saved my life.

After I had been sufficiently detoxed, I was shown to a room with two twin beds. My roommate had not yet arrived. I slowly realized that this was a recovery center that used the 12 Steps of Alcoholics Anonymous as a base teaching for a sober life. I always loved to read. When they gave me my copy of the Big Book, I devoured each page. I marveled at the insights and advice for a sane and healthy life. If only I had this manual years ago. I read that the founders of AA were Bill Wilson and Dr. Bob Smith, I thought what irony. My friend Dr. Bob is who I turned to for help.

My roommate arrived in the middle of our after-dinner meeting. She was asked to introduce herself to the group.

She said my name is Marianne and I am here for evaluation. Immediately, I was pissed off. I did not hesitate to identify as an alcoholic.

Once I was detoxed and could think clearly. I knew I was powerless and my life had become unmanageable. I had already done the second step when I called out to God to help me. The hard part would be turning things over to that higher power. I didn't like the idea of not being in control.

The next morning, we had a meeting and went around the room, introducing ourselves. Again, Marianne said she was there for evaluation.

I went looking for a counselor to talk to. Almost everyone that worked there was a recovering alcoholic. I found Nurse Jane and Counselor Lenny. Nurse Jane was a large woman and Lenny was a very short man. They made an almost comical picture. I told them about the anger I was feeling over my roommate's denial. I did not want to sleep in the same room with her. They tried talking to me but I was just too angry.

I went into the women's activity room and began to kick the furniture. I threw a few tissue boxes at the wall. Nurse Jane and Lenny came in and took me to a small room with one chair. There they were, my Mutt and Jeff couple on their knees reading to me from the AA Big Book. Then they gave it to me and had me read page 449 (latest edition changed to page 417).

"Acceptance is the answer to ALL my problems today. When I am disturbed, it is because I find some person, place, thing, or situation- some fact of my life unacceptable to me, and I can find no serenity until I accept that person, place, thing, or situation as being exactly the way it is supposed to be at this moment. Nothing, absolutely nothing, happens in God's world by mistake. Until I could accept my alcoholism, I could not stay sober; unless I accept my life completely on life's terms, I cannot be happy. I need to concentrate not so much on what needs to be changed in the world as on what needs to be changed in me and in my attitudes."

I grudgingly gave in and went to bed in the same room as Miss Denial. She was so afraid of me that she went to bed early and pretended to be asleep.

The next morning, she told me that if she said she was an alcoholic they would let her go home. So, at our morning meeting she said, “I’m Marianne and I am an alcoholic.” Then she left. However, we were destined to see each other again. She would turn out to be one of my many teachers.

# CHAPTER 46

# RELINQUISHING MY CROWN

All my coping defenses came out while I was in treatment. I immediately attracted a rehab boyfriend. He would come to my room at dinner time and escort me to the dining hall. Flirting was as far as it got but the need for male attention was undeniable. I formed a gal posse to hang out with and I was the leader. Need to control obvious.

There was a male counselor I found abominable. It may be because he resembled my ex-husband Jack in manner and appearance. Counselor Tim just rubbed me the wrong way.

After a brutally honest women's session. One of my gals was in tears. We were at the bottom of the stairs in the big meeting room. I was trying to console her. Tim came down the stairs and asked what was going on. I dismissively stated it was girl stuff. He replied, "Why don't you just tell me to go fuck myself?" Obviously, I rubbed him the wrong way as well. I reported his foul and aggressive language. He was reprimanded, which did nothing to improve our rapport.

I later learned that he bet someone $50 that I would not stay sober for more than a week after I left Marworth. I wish he made that bet with me. I would have saw his $50 and doubled it to $100. My validation came when I celebrated at a Marworth open AA Meeting, a year later.

I was only at Marworth about 10 days when the flowers started arriving, there were enormous bouquets from the Budweiser Salesman, Genesee Rep, and other tradesman I dealt with. Jerry wasn't aware of the concept of anonymity. He also had customers sign Get Well cards for me. I was quite the VIP in rehab.

Jerry tried to see me every day. The only way he could do that was by attending the public nightly meeting downstairs. The "inmates' would have to sit in the front row. After the meeting, he would sneak upstairs to the dining room. We would find a secluded corner to chat. Of course, we soon got caught and that ended that.

Most people were shocked to hear that I was in rehab. Jerry was the one that would pass out at the bar. I had never displayed public drunkenness. I would take pictures of him and do silly things to him when he got drunk. Put on goofy hats etc. He once passed out in Chick's Diner, his face landing in his mashed potatoes.

Yes, I was one of those "functional" drunks until I wasn't. My sessions with the psychiatrist and psychologist there educated me in Dual Diagnosis and Cross Addiction.

I had been self-medicating for years.

Many people diagnosed with a substance use disorder also suffer from a co-occurring mental health or behavioral disorder. This is known as a dual diagnosis. I was informed that my treatment plan needed to address both disorders as interconnected mental health issues.

The cross addicted diagnosis simply meant when one addiction is replaced with another. This can occur where the addict does not relapse on the same addictive behavior or substance, but instead, he or she becomes addicted to another substance or behavior. I had already had my struggles with men and food, so I knew I was in for the battle of my life.

I was also told that patients with this diagnosis pattern did not do well at staying sober. I promised myself that I would be the exception.

Jerry came up for a day visit when I was two weeks sober. We walked down the hill to the small lake. He proudly announced that he had stopped drinking. I told him that was a start but that we had to sell the bar. He blurted out, "What did they do to you in two weeks!"

I explained that Marie's Brier Patch had become my kingdom. I was the Queen and I ruled from my bar stool at the end of the bar. I was advised to give up my dominion or I would not stay sober. My happiness and well-being were based on abdicating my monarchy.

# CHAPTER 47

# CROSS ADDICTION

My husband went home and built a wall between the stairs leading to our apartment and the porch entrance to the bar. His declaration of sobriety consisted of drinking "Near Beers". Near beer is a malt beverage which does not contain enough alcohol to be considered a true beer. This beverage arose during the Prohibition in the United States, when alcohol was not permitted, but people still had a taste for it.

Alcoholics and people who struggle with substance abuse may want to avoid near beer, since it can trigger cravings, as it tastes a lot like beer, looks like beer, and is packaged like beer. The alcohol by volume (ABV) in a near beer may vary, depending on how it is brewed and handled. Generally, the ABV hovers around .5%.

When I told him, he was not truly sober, he wasn't happy. He reluctantly stopped drinking the "near beer". He was still tending bar along with our paid bartender Coz. When busy because of an event, we also still employed Mike and Joe. It was summer which is slow season for bars in Scranton. Every parish in town had a church picnic scheduled. That's where your business went in the summer.

I stayed out of the bar 90% of the time. If I saw a car I recognized, I might go down to say hello. One of these times, two customers were discussing a church picnic they wanted to go to. The problem was they did not know where it was located. It was not a church that they were familiar with. I got the phone book, looked it up and told them the address. One of them said "See what happens when you have a college degree?" I responded, "No, see what happens when you are sober." At that point my husband told me I was bad for business and threw me out. Barred from my own bar. How ironic.

My friend Dr. Bob had been admitted to Alina Lodge Rehab and Treatment Center in Blairstown NJ. His 28 day visits to rehab weren't doing the job. He was there for nine months .

My cross addiction got triggered in the form of food and spending. I had my own checking account and credit cards. I never added the balances up. I didn't want to know what the total owed was. I started gaining weight. By February of 1992 I had gained over 50 pounds.

I had married a wonderful man, graduated from college, and attained sobriety. Three enormous accomplishments. I had a sponsor, was going to meetings every day and working the steps. I also was in counseling. Would I ever be addiction free?

I came across a book called "It's Not What You're Eating, Its What's Eating You" by Janet Greeson, PH.D. When I finished the book, I learned that the author was also the founder and director of A Place for Us, a rehab in Los Angles, California. There was an 800 number which I immediately called.

I was currently looking for a job but had not found one yet. This seemed like perfect timing. My insurance would pay for everything. The rehab would pay for the airfare. When I presented this new chapter in my recovery to my husband, he was floored. I was 9 months sober and going away again. This time it was only 21 days.

I left for California the following week. When I landed there was a gal holding a sign with my name. She led me to the limousine. She opened the back door but I insisted I ride up front with her. As we drove through L.A. I was shocked at the amount of homeless people on the streets. When I arrived at the treatment center, the place looked very pleasant. The staff was very friendly.

I would live with mostly patients with eating disorders for the next three weeks. There was a girl with a sex addiction which proved interesting when her boyfriend came to visit. They were caught having sex in her room.

Unlike Marworth this place was very much like a spa. We had massage, meditation, light therapy, yoga, and other uncommon therapies. We also were taken on field trips to Venice Beach, Disneyland, and Long Beach.

We used to joke that they got our dinner from the lawn out front. We ate mainly a vegetarian diet six days a week. But Sundays we got to pig out. The theory was that you wanted to trick your body. Sunday, we ate high fat and high calorie foods. The theory being that our body would not know we were dieting.

By 1994 A Place for Us was out of business. A psychiatrist admitted falsifying patient records to trigger insurance payments. Dr. Greeson said she was the innocent target of a Blue Cross vendetta that has crippled her business, saddling her with personal losses of more than $1 million. She countersued the Blue Cross affiliates, charging that they had tried to ruin her by rejecting her clients' legitimate claims.

Weekend forays to recreation or shopping centers were billed as "life skills therapy." Twelve-step workshops were charted as "cognitive therapy" and aerobics classes as "physical therapy," according to the complaint.

To the basic accusation that A Place for Us used false medical diagnoses to obtain insurance payments, Greeson said: "It's a lie. How can I get all these psychiatrists to lie about a diagnosis? I have that much power? Nobody's going to put their credentials and license on the line for me."

The legal ramifications Janet Greeson was charged with had no impact on my experience at her rehab. She was a pioneer of this day-by-day self-help program. I addressed the physical, emotional and spiritual causes of my food addiction. I got in touch with my past and the feelings that triggered my eating problems. I learned significant information on food, nutrition, exercise, and stress management. My 21-day stay was an essential step in my growth. I was certain that I would have a new life, free of food addiction and depression.

**"Every great dream begins with a dreamer. Always remember, you have within you the strength, the patience, and the passion to reach for the stars to change the world." -Harriet Tubman**

# CHAPTER 48

# LIFE SKILLS

When I returned from California, I added up all my credit statements and sat down for a talk with Jerry. It was time to be brutally honest with myself and with him. We decided from now on there would be a joint bank account. The credit cards would be paid off and my accounts closed.

The food addiction was now in plain view. I tried to cut down on carbs and sugar. There was a 12 step meeting called Overeaters Anonymous. I went to one meeting. I felt like the group had an unrealistic approach to eating disorders. I never went back.

My college degree finally brought me some validation. I was offered a job at NEPA Center for Independent Living. It was as close to being a teacher as I ever thought possible.

Funded in part by the Commonwealth of Pennsylvania, Department of Labor and Industry, and Office of Vocational Rehabilitation, they connected people with disabilities with the independent living services they needed to enjoy greater freedom.

Mobility — wheelchairs, transfer devices, prosthesis, and walkers, Visual — screen readers, navigation assistance, braille embossers, screen magnification software, Hearing — hearing aids, assistive listening devices and amplified phone equipment Cognitive — educational software and memory aids.Services such as home modifications and assistive technology.

I would go and access the barriers holding them back to determine the services they needed to overcome them. I saw people of all ages and disabilities. Many young men with TBI, traumatic Brain Injury.

I met two women in a nursing home with Cerebral Palsy. They had been institutionalized for decades.

I was able to put together housing and communication technology that allowed them to move into their own apartments. Their families were not thrilled but my clients were ecstatic. One of them Sue was equipped with a laptop computer that she worked with a stick attached to a headband. The first thing she typed in was “People thought I was stupid but you helped show them I am not. You are my angel.”

Another client was a farmer who could no longer walk

and had grown greatly depressed. I was able to procure an agricultural electric wheelchair. It came with wide generous tread on the wheels. This type of wheelchair allowed him to check on his sons who were out in the field. Also, he could tend to matters such as pruning, milking, feeding, and caring for livestock, among other tasks.

Not every client was a success story. I found the young men with TBI to be the most challenging. One, was a paraplegic whose girlfriend had left him. He tried to commit suicide several times. One weekend, he succeeded by setting himself on fire in his apartment.

As rewarding as this job was, I was still newly sober. I had difficulty navigating the office politics. The office manager had a strong animosity toward me from the beginning. Backstabbing was her forte. She made a false accusation that I had insulted her. She demanded an apology. Her motive may have been jealousy. I do not know.

I was still in early sobriety and suffering from King Baby syndrome. King Baby Syndrome (or queen baby) was written by Tom Cunningham at the Hazelden Foundation in Minnesota. He wrote the pamphlet for recovering addicts and alcoholics to explore dry drunk syndrome. This term is obviously an oxymoron as it implies that a person is drunk without ingesting alcohol. Addiction is not about the substance it is an illness that results in a set of symptoms and behaviors that the substance medicates. Rather than apologize, I quit.

My experience at the CIL along with my degree in Health and Human Services made me very employable. I was hired at another center almost immediately.

The TRAUMATIC BRAIN INJURY CENTER was located in Clarks Summit. I was paid a lot more money. However, the clients needed more physical interaction than I was used to. I made it almost a year. Thankfully, the company went out of business and I was able to get unemployment benefits.

# CHAPTER 49

# QUEEN BABY

Jerry was not finding managing the bar alone a pleasant experience. We tried giving our bartenders more shifts. He just hated being there, now that he couldn't join in on swigging down drinks. The problem with neither of us being on the premises was all the rules were broken. The bartenders turned a blind eye to who went into the restroom and how long they were in there. The customers were doing coke in the lady's room. When cleaning one day I found all the cuts and nicks from cutting the cocaine.

Unlike the license from My Place, this license was a "moveable" one. Downtown Scranton was in the process of building The Steamtown Mall. An Italian restaurant was opening and they were looking for a liquor license. It was providential. We sold them our license and closed the bar.

Jerry was sad to see it go out of business but knew it was the only logical thing to do.

We tried running an AA Clubhouse on the first floor. A

Clubhouse is a non-profit facility that provides space for AA and Al-Anon meetings. Our vision was to create a safe and sober gathering place for fellowship and 12 step meetings. Each group meeting there paid a small fee for rent. As usual we were too successful. There were a lot of meetings including a motorcycle group. The noise from the parking lot was loud and profane. I think the neighbors would rather we still had the bar.

We tried enforcing rules regarding noise and loitering in the parking lot.

Eventually we had to throw in the towel. A good idea gone bad. We did some renovating and moved our main living area to the first floor. We were also to add an efficiency apartment. We had a total of six rentals.

A person with King Baby Syndrome can be both bossy and weak because of their childhood issues. A person with Queen Baby Syndrome will also act strong while feeling weak and depending on the validation of others. I was dependent on others in all sorts of ways, but I was doing everything to appear self-reliant. Just as a toddler can see a small misfortune as a terrible catastrophe, so can an adult with an immature personality.

When I couldn't control a situation, I would look for

one that I thought I could control. Aha, my weight! I was very unhappy shopping at Lane Bryant, the store for bigger women. The clothes were very nice but sizes went up to 5x or larger. The idea of needing that large of a size terrified me.

I decided to have bariatric surgery. This was the very surgery my friend Priscilla had in 1989.

Her friends including me, blamed that surgery for the heart attack that killed her shortly afterward.

I found a bariatric surgeon who did stomach stapling. This was 1994 and the more advanced safer procedures were still unknown. Your body mass index (BMI) had to be 40 or higher. This was about 55 pounds overweight for my body size. I missed it by 5 pounds. I started to cry and pleaded with the surgeon to please make an exception. After a pause, he said, “Oh, I misread your chart. I see that you are 55 pounds overweight after all.”

My husband was not at all happy about this newest plan of mine. He knew there was no changing my mind. The surgery was scheduled for the next week. I was excited. Something to focus on besides my character defects.

Unfortunately, there was a complication. After the surgery, I was not breathing well on my own. Intubation is required when general anesthesia is given.

The anesthesia drugs had paralyzed the muscles of my body, including the diaphragm, which made it impossible to take a breath without a ventilator.

Most patients are extubated, meaning the breathing tube is removed, immediately after surgery. I woke up with the tube still in. It felt like my throat was filled with cement. My wrists were tied and I could not speak. Panic engulfed me.

I wrapped my tongue around the tube and pushed it out with all the force I could. The medical staff was very upset with me. The surgeon said, "Well, if she could do that then I guess she didn't need the tube". I was very proud of myself. However, I could have done a great deal of harm to my larynx or the trachea.

I still had a problem with powerlessness.

After my bariatric surgery I lost some weight but not the 50-pound goal. This was becoming the focus of my control issues. Not being able to control the weight was sending me into deep depression.

In 1996 I filed for disability due to fibromyalgia, depression, and anxiety disorder. Dr. Lemon came to the hearing and testified that I was suffering from symptoms consistent with a diagnosis of major depressive order. My difficulties with concentration, memory, fatigue, and mood rendered me incapable of gainful employment of any kind. He also stated given my severe mood disturbances, I was a moderate risk for suicide. My disability was approved.

I threw myself into 12 Step work. I held many positions in local and state AA structures. AA general services included all kinds of activities within the Conference structure, district positions, area committees, delegates, trustees, the General Service Office and the Grapevine (A.A.'s monthly magazine).

I started a women's meeting with my sponsor Alvira. I sponsored as many as 10 women at a time. Jerry and I initiated a couples meeting and ran a couples retreat every year in the Poconos.

There was a newly formed Lackawanna Drug Court run by Judge Michael Barrese. He gave me the position of the women's Drug Court AA liaison. I was able to run weekend retreats funded by the county and focusing on the first three steps of AA.  I also ran a women's meeting every Monday at Marworth, my alma mater.

In was one of these Mondays that I ran into my nemesis from treatment. My ex-roommate Marianne. Remember she would not admit to being an alcoholic. Here she was five years later back in rehab, looking 20 years older. She did not hesitate this time to identify as an alcoholic.

I had worked the 12 Steps with my sponsors through the years. My first sponsor relapsed after 20 years in the program of Alcoholics Anonymous. My second sponsor moved out of town. Now my friend, Alvira and I were co-sponsoring each other.

I confided in Alvira that I had a resentment towards my father. Of course, I had many resentments but this one was more current. My dad claimed to have worked all the steps and was now sponsoring several young men. However, he had never done the ninth step with me. The ninth steps is the one where you make amends to those you hurt while in addiction.

Her advice was to write a list of all the perceived wrongs he needed apologize for. The list turned out to be a long one. I folded that list and put in my purse. In case, the opportunity should arise, I would be ready.

Resentments turn to anger, especially when unexpressed. I had not talked to my father in over a year. Then God intervened.

I had Jerry drop me off at an AA meeting. This meeting happened to be one block away from my parents home. The meeting had been cancelled. No cell phones at this time, so I was stranded. I had to walk to my parents' house to use their phone.

When I arrived there, my father was very surprised to see me. He hugged me and said, "You now that I love you, right?" I responded, "Maybe that's not enough."

He asked me what he could do to make it right between us. I reached into my purse and handed him the resentment list. He asked if he should read it now. I told him he could look at it later.

My father never did a formal ninth step with me. But I was free of the resentments. My ninth step to him was forgiveness.

I would get to see many friends and acquaintances at these meetings. I walked into the women's meeting room one day and was drawn to this particular girl. There she was balled up like a fetus in her chair. I walked over to her and was dumbstruck.

This was Priscilla's daughter. I spoke. “Dayna it's Marie, your mom's friend.” We were both very emotional and felt that her mother had done some heavenly maneuvers to have this happen. I became her sponsor that day. Unfortunately, she would be in and out of AA for several years.

Another surprise was interacting with a movie star. It was in the papers and the paparazzi were hanging outside the gates of the rehab. I'm not breaking anonymity as it was publicized. She herself talked about it in a magazine article.

I arrived at Marworth with my friend Joyce. We were having a coffee in the dining room. Joyce said that woman looks just like Kathleen Turner. I said it is Kathleen Turner.

She was very friendly and a willing participant in the group. I told her that my oldest daughter was a big fan. She said if I brought up a DVD next week, she would sign it. The following week I brought ROMANCING THE STONE and she signed it. She was in and out of recovery for many years. The last time she talked publically about her sobrierty was 2018.

I was also still in counseling myself. I was attending an AA meeting every day. The dual diagnosis part was not giving up. No matter how hard I worked on myself, the negative thoughts would come.

**"You don't have to control your thoughts; you just**

**have to stop letting them control you."**

**Dan Millman**

# CHAPTER 50

# MAGIC MOUNTAIN

The major causes of alcohol-related death are alcohol poisoning, cancer, car accidents, heart failure, liver damage, and violence.

By 1994 cancer had taken Jack Calvey at 47 years old. Coz McCormick died in 1999 at 40. 2001 took my sweet friend Joan 43 years old and Johnny Donahue age 51. Alcoholic deaths and funerals were an ongoing part of my life. That year I saw Marianne's obituary, my one-day roommate from Marworth. At least four people we knew committed suicide.

One of our customers, Pancho was found dead in his car. The week before another car he owned was set on fire. The death was considered suspicious.

Dr. Bob who had guided me to Marworth did not stay sober. He overdosed on a speedball (heroin and cocaine). He did not die but was in a coma for months. He sustained permanent brain damage. He lost his practice and his house.

We had more than one family member overdose on drugs. We tried to do interventions on a few family members and friends. Some just said no. Some went to treatment but left after a few days. Addiction is an insidious disease. No matter what your mind and your senses are telling you, the crafty tireless demon on your shoulder whispers the opposite.

Although, I was keeping drugs and alcoholism at bay, my depression was stealthily creeping back.

I had to tell my husband I needed inpatient treatment. This would be the third time I would need to go away and do some difficult inner work on my own demons.

I had survived my childhood by trying to be the "perfect child" and a caretaker from a young age. I was a child and yet I had to assume an adult role and take care of my siblings. From birth I had looked for acceptance and affection from a family that couldn't provide it. By the time I was five I knew it was never coming. The orphanage stay had planted the seed of being unworthy.

My father was an alcoholic who abused his family for years. My mother was a participant in that trauma. The hurt, shame and worthlessness were buried very deep. Getting sober was a good thing but it was also bringing back negative feelings from my core.

Even though I had a man who absolutely adored me, I was still insecure.

There was a program at the Caron Foundation that looked at your family of origin issues.

Richard J. Caron started out his adult life as an almost incorrigible alcoholic. He became a remarkable man and an inspiration to many. Thanks to his work, thousands have been forever changed at "Magic Mountain," the Caron Pennsylvania campus nestled in the eastern hills of Pennsylvania. They offered a five-day breakthrough program. They only took six or seven patients at a time. I applied and got in.

Caron's Breakthrough 5-day Program was set in a stunning mansion atop a hill. The 28-day treatment program was provided in the building at the bottom of that hill. We were bussed to that main building only for meals.

The workshop was meant to modify long-standing emotional and relational patterns that interfere with the client's quality of life or ability to function in day-to-day experiences. The methods included emotion-focused therapy, gestalt therapy, role-playing, mindfulness-based stress reduction.

One of the first things they had me do was write a letter to my inner child about abuse I experienced as a child. Then each person in the group read their letter aloud. Child abuse to me was cigarette burns, neglect, and sexual molestation. When I was writing my letter, I thought I did not fit the criteria. As I read my letter, I looked up to see one older woman crying. At the end, the counselor said, “You were absolutely a victim of child abuse.”

When we did the role playing, the older woman played my mother, the middle-aged man played my father and the young girl played me. I wondered if that was part of the criteria for who got picked for the week. They all fit their roles so perfectly. The father figure stood on a chair to accentuate his power. The “mother” cowered in a corner. The young girl knelt on the floor. The dark improv started with “Dad” yelling at the girl. One of the counselors started putting pillows on top of her. I was growing very anxious.

Without realizing it I started to retreat backwards. I looked over at “Mom” and she was crying and biting her hand. My back was now totally against the wall. They kept piling on pillows. I screamed “Stop” and ran to her. Tossing all the pillows until she was free. The symbolism was not lost on any of us. We then formed a circle and shared what we had felt and why.

Another exercise had to do with putting a voice to your repressed anger. Repressed anger can occur for many reasons, but traumatic experiences in childhood trauma are the most common culprit. After experiencing trauma, many people feel confused, sad, or ashamed, and blame themselves for what happened, causing them to internalize anger about what happened to them.

We each shared the end of a towel that was rolled up tight. The goal was to pull the towel out of the other persons hands. I gave a good fight but physical strength wasn't my strong suit. We then had a few minutes of silence. This session was becoming quite draining.

The counselor told us we were going to go deep and find our inner voice. When we found that voice, we were to give it permission to vocalize all the anger we had repressed through the years. Not wanting to be intimidated by the ability of my fellow patients to show their innermost anger, I volunteered to go first.

I closed my eyes. The therapist guided my thoughts to a cave and told me to picture going down into it. It was a deep fissure. It was icy cold and dark. I began to shiver. Intense emotions had always come to me in color. This time the color was deep purple. I let out a scream that was so powerful that I think some of my past lives may have joined in. When it was over, I opened my eyes. My fellow patients had a look of shock and awe. I hadn't really heard the scream. They told me it was blood curdling.

I could see how the use of these psychodrama exercises could be helpful. Because we tend to unconsciously recreate the old dynamics from our family of origin, the same old issues get played out again and again, either in romantic relationships or parent-child relationships.

I think I was attracted to Jack Calvey to re-create homeostasis (familiar order and organizing principles of the family of origin). And so "falling in love" with him involved providing that old familiar dynamic (no matter how painful or difficult) to "work through" my family of origin issues. Our relationship was an addiction. Although subconscious, there had always been a strange but powerful attraction to abusive men in my life. Along with the attraction was an irresistible desire to stay with these people even though things were going horribly wrong.

The counselors also illuminated the self-harm that I had inflicted as a way to deny the deeper pain. Excessive drinking, many "bad" men, cutting myself,over eating, violence and other risky behaviors.

If nothing else this five-day experience had shown me why I had accepted the unacceptable. I definitely had a hole in my soul. That phrase is used often in AA.

I had spent most of my life thinking power and control were needed to survive. Sometimes that was true. However, my need to control had only led to depression and several addictions. The need to control had been my way to deal with fear.

Pascal described human beings as having an infinite abyss which can be filled only with an infinite and immutable object; in other words by God himself. I was still searching for that elusive thing that would fill the empty hole.

The last 12 years of self-reflection had magnified my awareness that my true essence was unfulfilled. The Holy Grail that would lead me to joy, self- love and feeling connected to others was still to be discovered.

# CHAPTER 51

# SOUTHERN MIGRATION

The next few years were filled with the arrival of several grandchildren. They all loved coming to our house. We had taken over the entire first floor for our living area as well as part of the second and third floor for the girls' bedrooms. When they were grown adults, they shared that they thought we lived in a castle.

There was a separately deeded lot next to our building. We planted our first Christmas tree there as well as Pussy Willows and Cherry Trees. There was a flower garden and vegetable garden. The grandkids loved playing in the dirt with their little pails and shovels. As they got older, Frisbee and catch were the pastimes of choice. We felt young at 50. I am so thankful for the videos I have of those days.

We were still very involved with AA. That fall we planned our yearly couples retreat for the Poconos. As couples arrived, I would greet them and give them a room key and agenda. Suddenly, my right knee gave out. The rest of the weekend I was carried around in a chair by several of the men. Always a trooper, I still managed to direct most of the activities for the weekend.

On returning home, I made an appointment with an orthopedist. I needed a knee replacement. This would be the first of my many removals or replacements of bones and organs. I would go through at least twenty more surgeries in the next few years.

We were traveling every winter to Florida for a few weeks and then for the entire winter season. Jerry was able to take a sabbatical, which meant we spent three months in 2002- and three-months in 2003. Our snowbird place had always been Singer Island. Singer Island is a peninsula on the Atlantic coast of Palm Beach County, Florida. The town of Palm Beach Shores occupies its southern tip. Named after Palm Beach developer Paris Singer, a son of the Singer Sewing Machine magnate Isaac Singer, Singer Island has parks, marinas, hiking and bike paths, as well as 4.7 miles of white sand beach that has been considered one of the top five beaches in Palm Beach County.

We were able to find the perfect bungalow located on

Park Avenue and Blue Heron Boulevard. After crossing the main street, we would walk six blocks through a park before arriving at the beach.

Our landlords Dave and Wayne also had a beautiful inground pool. We were the only tenants allowed to use it. We became very good friends. Dave was on the City Council, so we were invited to many gala social events.

One of the most memorable was a jazz festival on the beach where Carlos Santana was the star act. Because his pioneering Latin rock band shared his surname, it's easy to conflate Carlos Santana with Santana, especially since the guitarist was the group's leader and spokesperson. Nevertheless, he also had an interest in collaborations with jazz musicians. That night we got to hear his jazz compositions.

Our return date to Scranton was usually before April 15. Partly because we had both a daughter and a granddaughter with that same birthday. April 2003, after a fantastic temperate winter in Florida, we were greeted at home with a foot of snow. I told my husband I just cannot spend the winter in Florida and return to an April winter.

We decided it was time to sell the house and move to Florida. Jerry could get early retirement at 55. I would turn 55 that October and would qualify us for senior housing.

I started to look on the internet for Senior Condo Developments.

A condominium is a building structure divided into several units that are each separately owned, surrounded by common areas that are jointly owned. Streets as well as any recreational facilities, are jointly owned and maintained by a community association. Instead of rent you paid a monthly fee for the maintenance of the land, buildings, and pools.

No longer worried about break-ins now that we had sold the bar, Jerry was going on his AA men's retreat on the Hudson River in New York., I asked him if I could sell the place while he was gone. He jokingly said of course. I wasn't joking.

I called my brother-in-law Charley who was a realtor. In a few hours he had a prospect. A guy from New York that was buying up all the multi-apartment buildings in town. I guess this guy had a vision of the change that was coming to Scranton. He came that day, and I gave him a tour of the building and property. At first, he gave me a low-ball offer. I told Charley to tell him no. Then I got the call that he would pay the asking price.

When Jerry called that night, I told him I sold the property. At first, he didn't believe me. Then he realized who he was married to. I asked him if he was happy about it. He responded that he was doing an Irish Jig in the hallway of St. Alphonsus. However he thought we should have discussed all the options first.

We brokered a deal with the new owner to let us stay till end of summer as a tenant. When summer ended, Jerry decided that for what it cost to move our furniture, we would be better off just buying new furniture in Florida.

I had my girls pick what they wanted. My oldest took the dining room set which made me very happy. The others took several items. We sold my grandfather clock to a neighbor that had always admired it. The adjustable bed I gave to someone who was very sick and could not afford to buy one. I felt good about that. We still had a lot of bar memorabilia in the basement. The next step would be a yard sale.

We put out the word that we would be having a three-day yard sale starting that Friday. It was mobbed that first day and we sold quite a bit. Jerry didn't want to bring what was left inside and then put it back out Saturday. He decided he would sleep outside to protect our belongings. With sleeping bag and baseball bat in hand, he began his night guard shift.

About 2 AM I heard a lot of yelling. I ran outside to see some guy scurrying down the street. He had been rummaging through our things. Jerry had run him off.

Saturday, we sold almost everything. The rest we gave away. I didn't want Jerry to spend another night outside. I had given all the photo albums to my oldest daughter for safe keeping. We still had a lot of personal things that filled our car from top to bottom.

We drove to our new home in West Palm Beach. The prior owner had left a bed, two recliners, a dinette set, chest of drawers and the appliances. So, we had the basics.

Our renovations would take almost two years. Tile floor instead of the carpeting. All new kitchen and both bathrooms. The previous owners had obviously done nothing since 1975 when they moved in. We were enjoying the remodeling. After all, compared to the renovations we had to do when Marie's Brier Patch almost burnt to the ground, this was a day at the beach.

We welcomed in 2004 quietly. Little did we know what was in store. Florida, was officially known as the "Sunshine State." It was dubbed the "Plywood State" by media after it was pommeled by four hurricanes in only six weeks. During the 2004 hurricane season. Nearly every square inch of Florida felt the effects from at least one of those four storms.

Hurricane Frances made landfall as a category 2 at Hutchinson Island on the Florida east coast.

The center of the storm was very large, 55 to 80 miles wide at landfall, but as the calm center passed overhead it belied what was to come as Frances moved inland. We were inexperienced with hurricanes, so we decided to leave.

We were driving to Wilmington, NC, where our military daughter Jenny lived. When we got to Jacksonville Florida, the weather alarm went off on the car radio. Tornado warning, get off the road now. We were fleeing a hurricane and now had driven into a tornado. It turned out that as the storm cut across the peninsula and moved on to the panhandle it created numerous tornadoes statewide.

We pulled into a motel and checked in to a room on the third floor. We hardly got in the room when the power cut off. We were in total blackness. Jerry walked down the two flights of steps to the desk. Each landing was lit with a lantern. They gave him a flashlight and a lantern for the room.

Three weeks later Hurricane Jeanne hit. Jeanne was a category 3 storm. Its 55-mile-wide eye crossed the Florida coast at virtually the same spot where Frances did. Widespread flooding rainfall of more than seven inches accompanied Hurricane Jeanne as it slowly moved west and north over the state. We stayed put this time. We had learned our lesson, shelter in place.

At that time the infrastructure of Florida did not have the capability to put in place alternative fuel sources. When a hurricane hit, traffic lights did not work. You could not get gas because the pumps ran on electricity. Restaurants for the most part were closed or had a restricted menu. After Hurricane Jeanne had passed through, we had a meal at Long Horn Steak House which was nearby. Their generator failed and the register didn't work. They told us the meal was on the house.

The Florida Legislature passed a law directing that certain gas stations along evacuation routes be equipped to switch to generator-based power, but most stations did not actually own generators. The law also required owners of eight or more fuel pumps in any one county to have access to at least one generator.

The 2005 Atlantic hurricane season was, at the time, the most active Atlantic hurricane season on record until the record was surpassed in 2020. Hurricane Wilma caused

$19 billion in damage and killed 30 people; five of the deaths were caused directly by the hurricane. Hurricane Wilma's storm surge caused the worst flooding in the Florida Keys since Hurricane Betsy in 1965. Wilma inflicted a multi-billion-dollar disaster in the Miami metropolitan area, including $2.9 billion in damage in Palm Beach County. We sheltered in place for all hurricanes that year and did not receive any damage to our condo.

Welcome to the Sunshine State.

# CHAPTER 52

# BUCKET LIST

I was a little bored. I started going to some AA meetings. We met lots of people. Before I knew it, I was sponsoring 5 women. My teacher nature was still the method I used to sponsor. Each gal had homework on the step she was on. We met once a week at my dining room table to go over the answers.

I started selling AVON . I had dabbled with selling cosmetics when I acquired my disability status. I went to nursing homes and doctors' offices. Soon I had over a hundred customers.

I joined the GLV Women's Club and met a lady named Dotty Levin, originally from Boston. She would become my closest friend. Dotty wanted to help people, that was her calling. She had a very big heart. Together we formed a group called Circle of Friends. It was an organization of volunteers to help all our Golden Lakes Village community. Our goal was to provide support for those who needed a little extra help in their daily lives. We did prescription pickups, gift Certificates for Food, Daily Check in Calls etc. Anything we could do to help those less fortunate than ourselves.

Jerry and I had a beautiful lake outside our back patio, where we would watch the sunset every night. Jerry would walk down and fish for hours. He was also swimming and playing golf. When we first moved to Florida, I was still cooking every day. My friend Dotty thought I was crazy. She said to me, "Do you know what Jewish women make for dinner?" I said no. She came back with "Reservations". I had to laugh. After that we ate out at least three times a week.

Now that we were retired, we also had a bucket list to work on. We took a trip to Maui and two trips to Italy. We walked through the ruins of Pompei, experienced the beauty of the Vatican and tossed coins into the Trevi Fountain.

Jerry went on a guided tour of Mt. Etna. He broke the rules and went behind ropes that signified danger. His friend Joe Gatelli got a great picture but Jerry got a scolding from the guide.

I was so grateful to have retired young enough to travel. We also took a car trip around the United States. June 01

2011, we left from Florida we traveled west to New Orleans. There were a few musicians on the street corners of the French Quarter. Not as many as I expected. We took a streetcar, the Red Canal Streetcar Line. It took us on a 5.5-mile route from the foot of Canal Street through the Central Business District and into the Mid-City area.

We then had coffee and beignets at The Du Monde Café ,established in 1862 in the New Orleans French Market. It is a traditional coffee shop. Beignets are square French -style doughnuts, lavishly covered with powdered sugar.

Maybe if we were drinking, we would have had a different experience in NOLA. I found it to be old, rundown and quite dirty.

The next day we drove to Little Rock Arkansas and checked into the Marriott Hotel. I wanted to visit the William J. Clinton Presidential Library and Museum and Park. I had a crush on Bill. Even though I had put a great deal of time and research into planning this trip, there were bound to be mistakes. I had not read that the Clinton Library was closed on Monday and Tuesdays. Of course, that is when we arrived on Sunday after 5 PM. We walked around downtown and had dinner and just had a day of rest.

Monday we headed to Graceland in Memphis, Tennessee. It was once owned by singer and actor Elvis Presley. His daughter, Lisa Marie Presley, has been the owner of Graceland since his death in 1977. We toured Elvis' house. The complex included an automobile museum, a Career Museum, the world's largest and most comprehensive Elvis Museum in the world. We also saw Elvis Presley's grave. He is buried on the grounds of Graceland, in the Meditation Garden that lies next to the pool.

The same day we left to visit my cousin Eddie Bauman in Colorado Springs Colorado. We stayed in their guest room for a couple of days. Eddie was a great tour guide. He ended up in Colorado because of his stint in the Air Force.

He took us to the U.S. Air Force Academy. The Cadet Chapel is the most recognizable building and the most visited man-made tourist attraction in Colorado. It is an aluminum, glass, and steel structure featuring 17 spires that shoot 150 feet into the sky. It is considered among the most beautiful examples of modern American academic architecture.

The next day was the Garden of the Gods. It is a registered National Natural Landmark. Imagine dramatic views, 300' towering sandstone rock formations against a backdrop of snow-capped Pikes Peak and brilliant blue skies. We ate lunch in the glass-enclosed café overlooking Pikes Peak. Jerry tried a buffalo burger. I did not.

We stopped in Las Vegas to see my niece, Jodi Tallo. She is quite an adventurous woman. She had worked for Richard Branson when she first got to Vegas. He paid well and eventually she bought a Pilates studio. In her spare time, she climbed mountains all over the world. I wish I had more than a day to spend with this admirable young woman.

We drove through Mt Zion Utah. Stopped at Mt Rushmore and then headed to Unity Village in Missouri. Unity Village just 15 miles from downtown Kansas City is the headquarters of our church. It has 1,200 wooded acres, the largest fountain display in the metro, an award-winning rose garden, and two buildings that are included on the National Register of Historic Places. The distinctive Mediterranean architecture creates a very tranquil atmosphere.

We stayed overnight in a rustic cabin. At dusk there were several deer right outside our window. Of all the places we visited in the United States, this was my favorite.

On the way home we visited Jerry's relatives in Cleveland and then headed to Scranton PA to see the rest of our families.

A 28-day adventure that we did not know would be impossible to do again. Both of us had major health problems that would start to limit our world.

# CHAPTER 53

# SEISMIC ACTIVITY

We were home and enjoying Florida life. Sitting on the beach and listening to the waves crashing. Jerry turned to me and said he was concerned about something. His left hand had been shaking a lot. I thought maybe it was Essential Tremor which is common in older people. We decided to see a neurologist as soon as possible.

We went to the Cleveland Clinic. The doctor's examination was very rudimentary. He had him walk down the hallway. When he came back to the exam room, the doctor proclaimed "You have Parkinson's Disease".

I had finally found happiness in my life and now this albatross had washed up on the beach.

Parkinson's disease symptoms may vary from person to person. Early signs may be mild. Symptoms often begin on one side of the body and usually get worse on the same side, even after symptoms begin to affect both sides.

Jerry's tremors were in his left hand. This was concerning

since he was left-handed. He was trying to wrap his mind around the fact that he had Parkinson's Disease. We saw more than one neurologist and finally came to accept the diagnosis. I was so grateful that we were both sober and had people to talk to an AA.

When we lived in PA, Jerry was in a golf league. His golf partner for many years was diagnosed with Parkinson's. The next day he went out into the woods and shot himself.

I knew I had to step up and be my husband's coach and cheerleader. From the moment he was diagnosed, I vowed to do the research, advocate for him, and make sure he did whatever was necessary to slow the progression of this disease.

Jerry was in Stage One which is mostly tremors on one side of the body. I started noticing his left foot was kicking out. I had also made note of the fact that he couldn't smell certain things. the earliest signs of Parkinson's are found in the enteric nervous system, the medulla, and the olfactory bulb, which controls sense of smell. He was put on Levodopa which is the usual medication prescribed.

That same year my father became very ill. A smoker most of his life, he had serious lung damage. He was on oxygen 24 hours a day. Each time he would be hospitalized, I had to decide if I should fly into see him. Every time, my mother would tell me he would be okay. He is not going to die . But this time, there was something in his voice that sounded different.

I booked the flight for the next day. In the morning , my brother Joe called to tell me Dad had passed.

My nephew Donnie and my brother handled all the details. Strangely, my brother Matt did not show up for the funeral.

Dad was laid to rest at Fairview Memorial Park in Elmhurst, PA. My mother asked me to pick up the framed memorial. On the way to get it we saw a rainbow. We got there and were handed the keepsake. We were stunned that the background behind my father's picture was that of a rainbow.

A few nights later we were back in Florida. I went to bed early. Jerry was watching TV. Suddenly, I felt as if someone had sat down on the bed. I sensed a strong energy presence in the room. I knew it was my father. I whispered, "It's ok Dad I forgive you."

Every time we see a rainbow, we feel that it is a beautiful, light-filled hello from my Dad.

My own health problems could be managed and I knew I needed to care of myself if I was going to take care of Jerry. Around the same time, my gynecologist discovered that I had a great deal of cervical polyps. He said it was more than he had ever seen and we should discuss how to proceed. My illnesses were never-run-of-the-mill.

I responded, "Just do a hysterectomy." Jerry was shocked that I decided that on the spot. The doctor asked if he could send a specimen to Johns Hopkins as it was extremely unusual.

So, I had a hysterectomy and carried on. That year, I was also diagnosed with Sjögren's Syndrome. Sjögren's is a systemic autoimmune disease that affects the entire body. Along with symptoms of extensive dryness, profound fatigue, chronic pain, major organ involvement, neuropathies, and lymphomas.

In 2015, Jerry's symptoms got much worse. Stage Two symptoms were manifesting. Tremor, rigidity, and other movement symptoms started to affect both sides of his body. Poor posture was very apparent. Daily tasks became more difficult. He had a hard time with buttons and shoelaces.

His Neurologist suggested Deep Brain Stimulation (DBS). In 2002 it had been approved for the treatment of advanced Parkinson's symptoms. In DBS surgery, electrodes are inserted into a targeted area of the brain, using MRI (magnetic resonance imaging) and recordings of brain cell activity during the procedure.

A second procedure is performed to implant an IPG, impulse generator battery (like a pacemaker). The IPG is placed under the collarbone or in the abdomen. The IPG provides an electrical impulse to a part of the brain involved in motor function.

Those who undergo DBS surgery are given a controller to turn the device on or off. Studies showing benefits lasting at least five years. That said, it is not a cure and it does not slow progression.

Jerry had the surgery and had to stay awake so that the doctors could test the correct neurons and map the brain. It took 8 hours and was a grueling day for both of us and our youngest daughter who came to be with us.

After recovering from the surgery, my husband rode his bike 8 miles every day and swam 66 laps in our community pool. He had the mind set of an athlete. He was determined to at least slow the progression. No walk into the woods for him!

**“Acceptance doesn’t mean resignation”**

**Michael J Fox**

# CHAPTER 54

# SOUL FOOD

Christmas 2013, I visited my mother in the nursing home. The nurses told me she was refusing water, food and medicine. When I entered the room, I was met with a ghost of the woman I knew. This was not the person I had seen on my last visit. I held her hand and asked her why she was rejecting food and water. She did not answer me. I asked her if she wanted to be with Dad. She shook her head no.

I knew my mother as well as I knew myself. She could be very stubborn. The last of her sisters had died a few months ago. Jane, the sister that had been in this home with her. The loneliness she felt must have been overwhelming. I knew my mother had decided to end her life and this unfortunately was the only type of suicide available to her.

I went home that night to my oldest daughter's house where I was staying for the holidays. I looked at her and said, "Trina, the next time I visit it will be to have Grandma's funeral."

She said I was crazy. She was holding on to the family denial that Grandma would live for many more years. She would not agree with my assessment of the situation.

My mother was in a shallow coma by January. My prediction had been accurate. For two days, I sat by her bedside. Her eyes were closed. She was hardly breathing. I rubbed lotion on her arms and hands. I brushed her hair. I talked to her about good family memories. I prayed out loud in case she could hear me.  I sat while other members of the family came to visit. She remained unchanged.

Finally, I asked my sister Ann if she had told her son how severe Mom's condition was. She had not. I called my nephew. I told him his grandmother was going to die.  That she was holding on until she saw all of her grandchildren. He was my parents favorite. They had practically raised him.

Even though he lived in another state, he was there in a matter of hours.  He entered the room and went to her bedside. As soon as he said Grandma, her eyes flew open. They closed almost immediately but it proved to me that he was what she had been waiting for.

We all went home that night expecting to take up the vigil the next day. Early, in the morning I got the call that she had passed. The nursing home said the mortician had already taken her body to the funeral home.

A few of us went to the nursing home to collect some of her belongings. Trina took the crocheted blanket from Hospice. The clothes would go to the Salvation Army. I chose a silver necklace and the journal "Mom, Tell Me Your Story," I had given her.

I was the executor of my mother's estate which was valued at minus zero. Thankfully, a few months before, I had paid the late payments on her life insurance. Her grandson Donnie and I met at the funeral home to make the arrangements.

My mother had in writing that she did not want a viewing. I arranged the church service with Nativity Church. The day of the service an arctic airmass moved over our area and produced a very cold and windy day.

My brother Matt did not attend the funeral nor did he see his mother the last few months of her life. Myself and my siblings have never found out why he completely detached from the family but I am sure he had his reasons.

I was still struggling with my weight. I saw an ad for lap band surgery at JFK Hospital. They stated that compared to other bariatric surgeries, the Lap-Band Program offered the safest, least invasive, lowest risk procedure, with the lowest rate of complications. The adjustable Lap-Band Gastric

Band is placed around the stomach to reduce its capacity. The resulting shape is like an hourglass, which helps promote a feeling of fullness, limits the amount of food that can be consumed at one time, and slows the movement of food from your stomach.

I made an appointment with the bariatric surgeon. A date was set for the placement. June 04 2014, I had the outpatient procedure and I went home the same day. I was supposed to fly up to PA in two weeks to visit family. However, I developed a fever and was told I had an infection from the lap band surgery.

July 03, the lap band device was removed from my digestive system. A pleural tube drain was inserted. They treated the infection with IV antibiotics. When one type didn't work, they put me on another. The one very powerful one caused me to lose control of my bowels. That was a humiliating day. I had a fever and shortness of breath.

A perfusion lung scan was performed using an injected perfusion agent. When they took me back to my room, I started to have a problem breathing. The technician had punctured my lung. I was placed on oxygen and air around the punctured lung was sucked out through a needle, allowing my lung to fully expand.

A CT was done of my abdomen and pelvis. It showed post-operative changes to my stomach. The upper quadrant showed inflammation and fluid. The final diagnosis was septicemia, septic peritonitis, trunk cellulitis, post op infection sepsis.

Days turned into weeks. I thought I was not going to ever leave there. Several of our church family came to visit me. We had joined Unity of the Palm Beaches when we moved here in 2003. July 12 2014, they discharged me with a picc line inserted into my chest. PICC stands for "peripherally inserted central catheter." This portal was inserted into my chest and below the shoulder. I needed to go daily for IV antibiotics.

I spent the summer in and out of JFK Hospital. Every time they would discharge me, my fever would spike and I would have to be readmitted. I was re-admitted July 25th. They did a small intestine endoscopy. The next six weeks I could not have food or water to prepare for the surgery needed to close a gastric fistula. A gastrointestinal fistula is an abnormal opening in the stomach or intestines that allows the contents to leak. Nutrition and fluid were delivered intravenously. All I could have was ice chips.

Surgery was performed to close the fistula. The surgeon

was also doing an abdominal paracentesis, a procedure to remove the fluid from abdominal cavity. The fluid was positive for contamination. After that surgery I developed pneumonia. While I was healing from the fistula closure, I was not allowed to eat or drink.

July 29 an EGD, an endoscopic procedure to examine my esophagus, stomach and duodenum was performed. This time the doctor found two more fistulas, inflammation of the esophagus middle compartment containing food remnants. Next day surgery was performed to close the fistulas. I was still on a liquid diet through an IV. The infection was still not under control.

I still had the PICC line in my chest for IV antibiotic transfusions. I had to go every day to the IV Infusion Center. That lasted for weeks. I finally thought everything was resolved. There was no fever so they closed the portal and gave me a final discharge.

I had spent at least 40 days with out food or water, just intravenous fluids. My stay at JFK was hell. The nurses were great but the disorganization and plethora of specialists were not.

The following year I started having trouble eating. I would throw up after every meal. All I could handle was crackers and water. I knew something was drastically wrong. I made an appointment with another gastroenterologist. He looked at my records and told me that there was someone more qualified for what was happening with me. He referred me to Dr. Robert Cwyes. Although Dr. Cwyes' main practice was bariatric surgery, he also specialized in the resultant complications that can happen.

Dr. Robert Cywes received his medical degree from the University of Cape Town Faculty of Medicine and has been in practice for more than 20 years. He had me stand behind an x-ray machine and drink water. Jerry and I watched the screen as water squirted sideways from my stomach. Dr. Cwyes scheduled me for a specialized endoscopy that would look at areas that were not usually examined. He said time was of the essence because of my symptoms. I would come back to his office two days after the test for the results.

When we arrived at Dr. Cwyes office three days later we were very apprehensive. He confirmed our worst fears. The past surgeries, stapling and the failed lap band and infection had severely damaged my stomach. He said there were holes where food could leak out, dead ends where food would stay and cause infections. I had more entero-enteral fistulas.

I needed to have most of my stomach removed and my gastro-intestinal system rerouted.

He also said that if I had waited a few more weeks to see him, I probably would have died.

The next day I had 85% of my stomach removed and portions of my colon. I was very depressed. My lovely minister, Rev. Taylor Stevens came to see me and I told him to leave. Fortunately, he hung out in the hallway with Jerry till I calmed myself. Then I asked him to come back in.

Our youngest daughter, Jennifer came to see me. She took a plane then the train and walked the last mile to the hospital. It was extremely hot that day. I didn't know till later of her laborious journey. Unwavering perseverance was part of her Marine training.

My nephew Brian came to see me. My sister Ann flew down to help. My friends and family called every day. I was finally discharged and went home with Ann and Jerry.

I had ordered an adjustable bed and had it waiting for me. I knew it would be a tough recovery. The bed would help with getting up in the morning and down at night. The next day I began to vomit mucous and fecal matter. The doctor told me to go to the ER immediately.

Jerry and I rushed back to the hospital. My dear minister was there when we arrived at the hospital to be with Jerry. By this time, my poor husband thought I was going to die. I had a blocked colon which meant another surgery.

Ann went home and Jerry's sister Rosemary came down to help us. I was unable to eat for a long time. Nothing tasted right. Finally, little by little I started to have a soft diet. It took me months to recover.

Dr. Cwyes told that I would be chasing nutrition the rest of my life. He gave me a diet to follow. As well as recommending B12 shots, multi vitamins and other supplements.

I thought about suing JFK but no lawyer would take the case. Some said it was a conflict of interest. Others said because I was already retired that there would be no basis for loss of income. Pain and suffering didn't matter.I just gave up trying to find a lawyer. I had survived everything life had thrown at me so far. Hopefully, I would survive this.

My relationship with food was forever changed. The pain and angst I endured for two years had decimated me.

**"Food for the body is not enough. There must be food for the soul." – Dorothy Day**

# CHAPTER 55

# JOYFUL ACCEPTANCE

January 30 2017, I had my yearly mammogram. Soon after I received a notice that I should have my doctor order an MRI. I did and they found a small mass in my left breast. Next was two more tests, a more precise digital Mammogram, and a biopsy. We came for the results on March 17, St. Patrick's Day.

Jerry and I walked into Dr. Goodwin's office in Palm Beach Gardens. He had the picture on his computer showing the mass. He looked up from his desk and did not beat around the bush. He declared "It is definitely cancer." He then proceeded to explain how the cell structure was different than normal cells, I wasn't listening. I was already thinking about the next step.

April 6th, I met with the breast surgeon Dr. Minnick. She thought we might be able to do a lumpectomy. However, she needed me to have further tests done. I then had an MRI of both breasts.

The next visit she informed that I had HER2-positive breast cancer, a breast cancer that tests positive for a protein called human epidermal growth factor receptor 2 (HER2). This protein promotes the growth of cancer cells.

She asked if we could wait a few minutes since she had not received all the images. We did. Fifteen minutes later, she called us back into her office.

The other images revealed that there were two tumors not one. That meant that a lumpectomy would not be the preferable way to go. Mastectomy was then discussed. I told her to do a double mastectomy.

After we left, Jerry said, "Don't you think we should have discussed all the options first." I said I am not taking any chances and I was not going to walk around with only one boob. My body, my choice.

I consulted with my plastic surgeon and decided to start reconstruction parallel to the mastectomy.

May 18, Dr. Minnick removed both breasts and some lymph nodes that were tested on the spot. My plastic surgeon, Dr. Kapp inserted extenders that would stretch the skin for the implants. I went home the next day with four drains.

My oncotype score was low enough that I didn't need chemotherapy or radiation. Oncotype DX, is a diagnostic test that estimates the likelihood of disease recurrence in women with early-stage hormone estrogen receptor positive breast cancer.

My oncologist Dr. Mewar put me on Arimidex. This is used to treat breast cancer in women after menopause. Some breast cancers grow faster by the hormone estrogen. Arimidex decreases the amount of estrogen the body makes and helps to slow or reverse the growth of these breast cancers. One of the side effects is bone loss. That meant I had to get a Prolia shot twice a year. The Prolia caused side effects severe enough that the doctor stopped them and switched me to Tamoxifen.

The first set of implants were not symmetrical and had to be replaced. I then developed RBS "Red Breast Syndrome". My left breast, the one that had the tumor turned completely red. Dermal matrix also known as acellular dermal matrix (ADM) is a tissue product harvested from a cow. This biological tissue bonds as new blood vessels form and the tissue becomes part of the patient's breast pocket.

However, a small percentage of women have an adverse reaction. Studies now show some patients experience this specific complication called red breast syndrome (RBS), and it has been linked to ADM use. I guess I'm allergic to cows. My plastic surgeon told me take Benadryl. The redness never went away.

I had three more surgeries to deal with seromas, infections, and asymmetry.

There is a growing concern the breast implants can cause auto immune diseases. Breast Implant Illness {BII} can occur with any type of breast implant, including silicone gel-filled, saline-filled, smooth surface, textured surface, round, or teardrop-shaped.

Symptoms can include: joint and muscle pain chronic fatigue, memory, and concentration problems rashes and skin problems, dry mouth, and dry eyes anxiety and depression. I could check every box.

Also having been diagnosed with Sjogren's Disease, it was obvious the implants had to be removed. July 3 2021, I went flat and I have never felt better. After four years of being sore, tired, and lop-sided, I had the implants removed.

I joined a group online called Flat, Fierce and Forward. Women who opted to go flat. Through this group I have learned how prevalent Breast Implant Illness is. I wish I knew more about BII, four years ago when I chose re-construction instead of an aesthetic flat closure.

**"You wake up every morning to fight the same demons that left you so tired the night before, and that, my love, is bravery." – unknown**

# CHAPTER 56

# MODERN MEDICINE

Stage 3 is the middle stage in Parkinson's, and it marks a major turning point in the progression of the disease. Jerry was now experiencing loss of balance and decreased reflexes. His movements became slower overall. Falls become more common. His daily bike ride often resulted in antibiotic ointment and bandages.

Fishing, his favorite hobby ,was now impossible. He tried to get up from his fishing chair and fell over. It took more than a few minutes to right himself. I couldn't see him from the patio since he had gone down the embankment and close to the water. That was his last day of fishing.

His brother Jim came to visit and they went to play a round of golf. After that, golf became a sport that he watched on TV. His clubs gathering dust out back with his fishing gear.

The bike riding continued. I begged him to get a stationary bike to ride in the house. He was stubborn. One day he fell into our garden on top of some stone flower pots. I couldn't stop the bleeding and had to take him to the ER. He got several stitches in his knee and arm. That Christmas there was a stationary bike under the tree. The outdoor Schwinn joined the corner of unused sports equipment.

He was still adamant about slowing the progress of this damn disease. He diligently rode the exercise bike every day for two to three miles. Some afternoons, he also would go for a swim. He liked the smaller pool which was just for our street. The problem was he was often the only one there. I wanted him to swim at the Clubhouse Community Pool where there were always people around. If I was going to swim with them then we could go to the smaller pool.

He was careful sometimes and sometimes he was not. One of the days he went to the smaller pool without telling me. He came home bloody and bruised. He had tried to get out from the deep end using the ladder instead of the shallow end with the handrail. Of course, he lost his balance and fell head first. His knee, left forearm and forehead were badly bruised. He promised to go to the Clubhouse pool from then on.

Unfortunately, his fatigue began to worsen. Many people with Parkinson's disease experience extremefatigue.

The fatigue can be caused by or made worse by muscle stiffness, depression, changes in being able to move or sleep well. Jerry had all those symptoms. He started to go to the pool less and less.

He tried to be helpful around the house. One day he washed the floor in the front entry way. He neglected to tell me and when I came out of the bedroom, I slipped and fell. I did a full split which I didn't think was possible. I jammed my left shoulder on a trunk that was in the corner of the room. I could not move. I told him to call an ambulance. I had to tell him three times before he made the call. I had broken my shoulder.

My main thought was who is going to take care of him. I had the first shoulder surgery and it was unsuccessful. I sought a second opinion and found an orthopedist who told me he could help me. He would do a reverse total shoulder replacement.

In a reverse total shoulder replacement, a surgeon removes the rounded head of the upper arm bone. Using screws and special tools, he or she attaches a plastic socket to the remaining bone. The surgeon also removes part of the socket of the shoulder blade. This is then replaced with a metal ball. The metal ball can then move around inside the socket that attaches to the upper arm bone.

At this point I had two knee replacements, left and right knee and now metal in my shoulders. The Xray machines at the airports also picked up loose staples floating around from by failed bariatric surgery. From now on, I could never get through airport security without a pat down.

Even with all my medical issues I still feel blessed every day. I am alive and loved.

My friend Marlene, one of the Capitol girls called me in August 2019. She was crying hysterically and finally calmed down to tell me why. Dayna, Priscilla's daughter had been killed while riding her moped. Police found a connection to the possible location of the car involved in the crash. A Dodge charger was found in someone's garage, but the owners were not cooperating. Florida Highway Police found her moped on Sandridge Road at 2:20 a.m. They believe it was rear-ended. Troopers are trying to piece together how her body ended up more than 8 miles away.

She had finally found sobriety only to be killed by a drunk driver.

**"It does not matter how long you are spending on the earth, how much money you have gathered or how much attention you have received. It is the amount of positive vibration you have radiated in life that matters,"**

**— Amit Ray, Meditation: Insights and Inspirations**

# CHAPTER 57

# PIROUETTES AND PROGRESSION

Early in March 2020 we went on a cruise with our granddaughter Vanessa and her fiancé. We had no idea what was happening with the approaching pandemic. It is a miracle that none of us got the Covid-19 virus.

Mid-March my grandson Joey came to visit. The news that this was destined to be a pandemic was out. I arrived to pick him up at the PBI airport wearing surgical gloves. We did not know yet how the virus was spread. He thought I looked like a crazy woman.

I explained to him that the night before a traveler arrived at PBI airport and tested positive for the virus.

They had closed down that terminal and sanitized everything. The virus was beginning to spread quickly. Many restaurants and other businesses closed.

We got to take my grandson to one outdoor restaurant before they were advised to shut down. March 17, I took him back to PBI and then voluntarily isolated with Jerry for a year.

I had to lay off my cleaning lady, Tina who came twice a month.  Later on although vaccinated she became affected with Covid. We both were having massage therapy and we had to suspend that. A few months later my masseuse Alexandra caught Covid from her 14 year old daughter.

No one allowed in and we were not allowing ourselves to go out. Like everyone else our lives were in Limbo. Zoom and Facetime were our new communication tools. I did a lot of organizing and remodeling in the condo. We started getting our groceries delivered. I upgraded to a Prime Amazon membership for the free delivery feature.

Jerry's PD progression had noticeably progressed. He was still able to walk and stand unassisted, but he was noticeably declining. He refused to even consider using a walker. I had physical therapists, speech therapists and occupational therapists lined up for him. Mostly on Zoom and just the occupational therapist in person at our home. We all wore masks when she was here.

Up till now, Jerry thought swimming and riding the stationary bike everyday was enough. I knew he needed more. He needed some assistive devices to live an independent life. After all, that had been my last job, an Independent Living Counselor.

I had to just go ahead and order what he needed. I ordered grab bars for the toilet in his bathroom and a shower chair. I bought a lift chair to help him get in and out of the recliner. Our dining chairs were armless when we bought them almost 20 years ago. I was focused on fashion not function. Every time he got up from the table, he would lose his balance and do a pirouette like a ballerina. I ordered two dining chairs with arms.

Every one of these purchases were met with disdain and denial. Every one of these items proved very useful. My need to feel in control was manifesting in this situation. I did not want to admit I was powerless.

The pandemic combined with his progression had elevated my depression and anxiety levels. I found myself feeling resentful and being downright mean to him. Luckily, I recognized what was going on with me and got help.

First, a psychiatrist that asked me what I took for depression and for how long. I told her I had been on the same dosage of Zoloft for 3o years. She informed me that I had built up a tolerance and promptly doubled my dosage. She also told me to take low dose valium every afternoon about

1 PM.

I started counseling with a psychologist on Zoom which was very helpful. After a week or two, I was no longer mean to my husband. I was still pretty pissed off at the disease though.

Jerry was also accumulating a myriad of dents and scratches on our car. Parkinson's disease can significantly impair driving skills, cause safety concerns, and force many people with the condition to stop driving a car. Sone symptoms of Parkinson's disease can interfere with the complex task of driving a car. These symptoms are tremor, rigidity, slowness of movement, and impaired balance. In addition, some people with Parkinson's disease may develop cognitive impairment, defects in thinking, language, and problem-solving.

His neurologist told him he had two choices. He could buy a new car with all the safety features, blind spot alert, back up camera, automatic braking etc. The other choice was to wait till he had a car accident and then Dr. Dalvi would be legally mandated to report his PD to the DMV and he would lose his license.

He still dragged his feet, literally and metaphorically. After a few weeks, I did research on the best car for him to be able to drive safety. I researched the trade-in value of our current car. I made the appointment with the car dealer. He went but was not happy about it. He said, "I will not be pushed into buying a car. Don't expect to leave with a car today." We bought a 2018 Sonata with all the safety features. We got more of a trade-in than he expected and a seven-year warranty. I could finally breathe and felt some of the stress I had been carrying leave my body.

Around 60% of people with Parkinson's disease fall at least once a year, with a large proportion (50-86%) falling multiple times in this period. My husband was falling every few weeks. Sometimes in the house and sometimes outdoors. He adamantly refused to even consider a cane or a walker.

I called his physical therapist who he was now seeing onsite at the facility. I asked her if she had done a Berg scale on him. This was a way to calculate the predictably of falling. She said, "No but every week I ask him if he has fallen and he always says no." I told her he was lying.

His next appointment she conducted the Berg test. His score was 37. A score below 40 indicates risk of falling as a predictive probability, without doubt. This low of a score indicated a cut-off for safe independent ambulation and the need for assistive devices.

The therapist and I agreed he should get a rollator. The rollator helps to offer stability and balance to the user so that they don't need to worry about staying upright or supported. Because they have wheels, rollators can help people who may have limited strength, making it much easier to push the rollator forward. I told her to check our insurance and order it sent to the facility so she could train him the correct way to use it.

Presently Jerry has a difficult time rising from a chair and getting in and out of bed. He loses his balance quite often when standing or turning, and sometimes freezes or stumbles when walking.

I am always on alert when he gets up from a chair or turns too quickly. I also have noticed memory problems and slowness of thought.

The good news is most people with PD never reach stage five. I am keeping a positive attitude and a prayer in my heart that he is one of those people.

# CHAPTER 58

# THE LESSON

One of the first places I visited when I moved to Florida was the Loggerhead Marine Life Center in Juno Beach. LMC is committed to the rehabilitation of sick and injured sea turtles. In the souvenir shop I was drawn to a hand carved wooden turtle . I immediately felt this was my spirit animal.

The turtle's hard shell is an analogy for endurance , perseverance and also the idea that what doesn't kill you makes you stronger.

The spiritual meaning of a turtle is finding the way to move forward and live through heavy times. As the turtle is a slow pacer, so was my spiritual enlightenment .

I spent a great deal of time trying to find the meaning of life. It took decades to realize that my purpose in life could not be found in my mind.

It was a living body that existed in me that I was not even aware of. The Shaman Ruda' lande' said the greatest experiences come from our actions not our feelings. The same can be said about purpose. You don't need to know your purpose to have one. Our actions towards others defines both meaning and purpose.

When I allowed myself to be instead of trying so hard to do all the time, I was finally able to hear my true inner voice. I started noticing all the synchronicities in my life. Every path I took, even the detours, had been defining my unique intention in life. My purpose showed up through my actions whenever I tried to help others.

Eckhart Tolle stated that the it's not the things that happen to you that your pain arises from, but your response to it.

For years my response was to be a survivor, a mother warrior, and an ice queen. Unfortunately, playing those roles resulted in emotional numbness. My heart was sealed shut. I became emotionally numb to protect myself from further emotional and physical pain.

I became unable to cry. I lost the ability to feel sadness. Becoming emotionally numb was not a conscious choice. However, it protected me from uncertainty, risk, and vulnerability. Emotional numbness often occurs as a coping mechanism, a way of blocking out painful experiences and emotions.

I had been through a lot in my life. My mind needed a break. The lack of emotional responses from my parents during childhood combined with the dysfunction of a violent alcoholic home caused me to have selective amnesia regarding most of my childhood. Then as an adult, I started to switch off both negative and positive emotions.

Human beings are meant to feel emotion. When that mechanism is short-circuited, first by emotionally neglectful parents and later by bad choices as an adult, it throws off the whole organism. Depression and anxiety are two of the most common causes of emotional numbness. Trauma and addiction were also on my personal hit parade.

I had to hit bottom emotionally, physically and spiritually. I had to ask for help. I had to get sober. Many years of counseling, soul searching and gut-wrenching honesty have started to dissipate that numbness.

I was able to break free from my demons. I no longer felt trapped. I still only cry when I am angry or frustrated. I do have moments of happiness but not necessarily joy. Progress not perfection is my maxim.

What I have learned from my life is that the human spirit is strong and can overcome almost anything.

I also believe we each have a major pattern to resolve

in our lifetime. I have spent a major portion of my life uncovering, forgiving, and resolving that pattern.

I still have a lot to learn and discover about life, love, joy, and my true self. Today my heart is open. I look forward to continuing the journey.

**"You are a divine being. You matter, you count. You come from realms of unimaginable power and light, and you will return to those realms."**
**Terence McKenna**

# EPILOGUE

I started this story relating that I grew up in a predominantly Italian household. My father hated that his biological mother was Irish . Christmas 2019, I received an Ancestry DNA kit as a gift from my husband. The results were shocking. I learned that my father was 100% Irish. After tracing the line through my DNA matches, I found I had a first cousin who lives in Texas. Upon contacting her , it was also revealed that her father was his half-brother. His biological parents were James Scanlon and Catherine Quinn of Scranton. There were also hundreds of DNA matches from one area, County Mayo, Connacht Ireland. First, second and third cousins! I still have further discovery to do and resolution to perform regarding my Irish family. Now I know I have a Gaelic blood line, that goes back hundreds of years. What I discover about that branch of the family will be the subject of my next book.

# AFTERWORD

The stories in this book reflect the author's recollection of events. Some names, locations, and identifying characteristics have been changed to protect the privacy of those depicted. Dialogue has been re-created from memory.

# ACKNOWLEDGEMENT

I wish to personally thank the following people for their contributions to my inspiration and knowledge and other help in creating this book:

My brother, Joseph Tallo and my sister Ann Tallo for filling some of the holes in my memory.

Rev. Taylor Stevens for the daily inspiration I gleaned from his sermons.

The late Bonnie Glover, a candid and veteran author who guided me on the minutiae of book publishing.

My loving husband Jerry Brier for weathering the storm with me all of these years.

# ABOUT THE AUTHOR

## Marie (Mimi) Tallo Brier

Marie was born in Scranton, PA in 1948. She grew up on the South Side of town. She has worked since she was a young girl as a cocktail waitress, bartender, medical assistant,insurance-underwriter, business owner and a counselor for the disabled.

She graduated from University of Scranton with a BS in Health and Human Services. Marie was a Living Skills Facilitator working with the disabled and teaching life skills to adults with TBI (traumatic brain injuries) and Cerebral Palsy. After retiring, she served as the Women's Liaison in the Lackawanna County Drug Court. She acted as Co-Ordinator for Unity of the Palm Beaches prayer chaplains. Marie is co-founder of "Circle of Friends", a group of volunteers helping the elderly in her community. She is currently working on her next book, "Pentimento, Uncovering my Irish Ancestry."

# PRAISE FOR AUTHOR

*Marie looked at her life head on and decided to do something about it. This is a sign of a rational, wise person who takes responsibility for themselves. She also applied the same approach to healing her body. In both cases she turned up a winner. There is much to be learned by reading her book. Congratulations!*

*Alice McCall Author*
*Cellular Level Healing*
*President, Healing Path*

*I never realized that Marie had gone through so many traumatic experiences. It was enlightening to learn how she escaped the hostile and violent environment of her past. The woman I know today is committed to living a life with purpose and love.*

*Josette Veltri Author*
*Next Steps & New Starts: Baggage*

# BOOKS BY THIS AUTHOR

## Raised By Wolves Trapped By Demons

A major portion of my life has been spent uncovering, forgiving, and resolving my self-destructive patterns. I wrote this book for the still marginalized women in this world. I have been a victim, a survivor and today an imperfect but integrated spiritual being. Putting on paper the bare unadorned truth of my life is both frightening and freeing.

## Pentimento Uncovering My Irish Roots

Publishing Date TBA

REFERENCES


https://en.wikipedia.org/wiki/Meadowlark_Lemon

http://mafiahistory.us/maf-b-sc.html

https://thenewyorkmafia.com/2021/03/18/the-bufalino-family-of-northeastern-pennsylvania-men-of-montedoro/

https://en.wikipedia.org/wiki/Maslow

https://en.wikipedia.org/wiki/History_of_anthracite_coal_mining

https://www.thetimes-tribune.com/opinion/editorial/...

https://www.mylife.com/william-cerra

https://infogalactic.com/info/Bufalino_crime_family

https://www.imdb.com/name/nm0588553

https://mafiahistory.us/mafiahistoryblog

https://world-nuclear.org/information-library/safety-and-security/safety-of-plants/three-mile-island

https://en.wikipedia.org/wiki/
Wilson_College_(Pennsylvania)

https://beyourownbrandofsexy.com/meet-dr-susan-edelman

https://www.healthline.com/health/relationships/
hysterical-bonding

https://www.alinalodge.org/

https://www.answeraddiction.com/kathleen-turner-talks-
alcoholism-recovery/

https://worldbirds.com/turtle-symbolism/#power

Made in the USA
Columbia, SC
08 October 2021

46922606R00250